Redefining
STUDENT
ACCOUNTABILITY

A Proactive Approach to Teaching Behavior Outside the Gradebook

TOM SCHIMMER

Solution Tree | Press
a division of
Solution Tree

555 North Morton Street
Bloomington, IN 47404
800.733.6786 (toll free) / 812.336.7700
FAX: 812.336.7790

email: info@SolutionTree.com
SolutionTree.com

Visit **go.SolutionTree.com/behavior** to download the free reproducibles in this book.

Printed in the United States of America

Library of Congress Cataloging-in-Publication Data

Names: Schimmer, Tom, author.
Title: Redefining student accountability : a proactive approach to teaching
   behavior outside the gradebook / Tom Schimmer.
Description: Bloomington, IN : Solution Tree Press, 2023. | Includes
   bibliographical references and index.
Identifiers: LCCN 2022047349 (print) | LCCN 2022047350 (ebook) | ISBN
   9781952812132 (paperback) | ISBN 9781952812149 (ebook)
Subjects: LCSH: Motivation in education. | Effective teaching. |
   Professional learning communities.
Classification: LCC LB1065 .S363 2023 (print) | LCC LB1065 (ebook) | DDC
   371.39/3--dc23/eng/20221129
LC record available at https://lccn.loc.gov/2022047349
LC ebook record available at https://lccn.loc.gov/2022047350

Solution Tree
Jeffrey C. Jones, CEO
Edmund M. Ackerman, President

Solution Tree Press
President and Publisher: Douglas M. Rife
Associate Publishers: Todd Brakke and Kendra Slayton
Editorial Director: Laurel Hecker
Art Director: Rian Anderson
Copy Chief: Jessi Finn
Senior Production Editor: Suzanne Kraszewski
Copy Editor: Jessi Finn
Proofreader: Mark Hain
Text and Cover Designer: Julie Csizmadia
Acquisitions Editor: Hilary Goff
Assistant Acquisitions Editor: Elijah Oates
Content Development Specialist: Amy Rubenstein
Associate Editor: Sarah Ludwig
Editorial Assistant: Anne Marie Watkins

Acknowledgments

Solution Tree Press would like to thank the following reviewers:

Kim Freiley
English Language Arts Teacher
Ingersoll Middle School
Canton, Illinois

Elizabeth Love
Principal
Spradling Elementary
Fort Smith, Arkansas

David Pillar
Assistant Director
Hoosier Hills Career Center
Bloomington, Indiana

Sheryl Walters
Instructional Design Lead
Calgary, Alberta, Canada

Steven Weber
Associate Superintendent for
Teaching and Learning
Fayetteville Public Schools
Fayetteville, Arkansas

Bryn Williams
Principal
Coquitlam School District
Coquitlam, British Columbia,
Canada

Visit **go.SolutionTree.com/behavior** to download
the free reproducibles in this book.

Table of Contents

Reproducibles are in italics.

About the Author

 **Tom Schimmer** is an author and a speaker with expertise in assessment, grading, leadership, and behavioral support. He is a former district-level leader, school administrator, and teacher. As a district-level leader, he was a member of the senior management team responsible for overseeing efforts to support and build the instructional and assessment capacities of teachers and administrators.

Tom is a sought-after speaker who presents internationally for schools and districts. He has worked extensively throughout North America, as well as twenty other countries. He earned a teaching degree from Boise State University and a master's degree in curriculum and instruction from the University of British Columbia.

Tom is the author and coauthor of multiple books, including *Growing Tomorrow's Citizens in Today's Classrooms: Assessing Seven Critical Competencies*; *Standards-Based Learning in Action: Moving From Theory to Practice*; *Instructional Agility: Responding to Assessment With Real-Time Decisions*; *Essential Assessment: Six Tenets for Bringing Hope, Efficacy, and Achievement to the Classroom*; and *Grading From the Inside Out: Bringing Accuracy to Student Assessment Through a Standards-Based Mindset*.

To learn more about Tom's work, visit http://allthingsassessment.info or follow @TomSchimmer on Twitter.

To book Tom Schimmer for professional development, contact pd@SolutionTree.com.

Introduction

The social and emotional factors in learning are the core, but attention to them remains painfully uncommon in the debates about school reform.
—TIMOTHY P. SHRIVER AND JENNIFER BUFFETT

Using grades to coerce students to comply with behavioral expectations is a practice so traditional in schools that it often goes unchallenged. When educators threaten to penalize students for late work by dropping them a letter grade, for example, they see this as a way to both punish students and to provide an incentive for students to meet the deadline—they use the threat of a reduction of the academic score to compel behavioral compliance. Teachers philosophically defend this practice, parents don't question it, and students accept it. The definitiveness with which some educators use their gradebooks for behavioral incentives and consequences can make it seem like the only option for teaching students to be accountable for their behavior.

Those who advocate for using grades as behavioral management tools, and who feel that students deserve penalties when they don't act responsibly, commonly argue that "educators need to prepare students for life in the real world." The penalties are "for their own good" and "important life lessons." While preparation for life after school is a noble cause, admonitions such as, "Wait until you enter the real world" disrespect and dismiss students. Adults in schools tend to draw a fictional line between the student world and the adult world. But students do live in the real world.

The Real World of Students

The human brain doesn't reach full adult faculties until one's early to midtwenties (Dobbs, 2011; Wnuk, 2018). Some of the main differences between the adult brain and the adolescent brain lie in the development of the prefrontal cortex, the part of the brain responsible for planning, solving problems, and making decisions (Wnuk, 2018). Adolescent brains tend to be influenced more by emotion, reward, and social acceptance. No matter how hard adults try to force students to display adultlike behavior, they cannot force physiological development or the capacity for adult rationalization.

In addition, data reveal that the world students inhabit is filled with pressures and difficulties as daunting as those in the world of adults, like those challenges that poverty can bring. Consider the statistics from the United States and Canada in figure I.1.

UNITED STATES	CANADA
• One in seven American children live in families whose income is below the federal poverty threshold (11 million; Organization for Economic Cooperation and Development, 2021). • Forty percent of American children will spend at least one year in poverty before the age of eighteen (Ratcliffe, 2015). • The high school dropout rate among students from low-income households is 11 percent (compared to 3 percent for high-income households; McFarland, Cui, Holmes, & Wang, 2020).	• Twenty percent of Canadian children live in poverty. • Fifty percent of First Nation–status children live in poverty. • Forty percent of Indigenous children live in poverty; 60 percent of Indigenous children who live on a reservation live in poverty. • Thirty-three percent of all people who access food banks across Canada are children. (All statistics from Canada Without Poverty, n.d.)

Figure I.1: Poverty and the real world of students.

The challenges that students and families who live in poverty face are very real, such as food insecurity, access to stable housing, access to stable employment, and access to resources. Let's now examine some relevant statistics about the mental health and wellness of children and youth in Canada and the United States (see figure I.2).

UNITED STATES	CANADA
• An estimated 20 percent of students ages twelve to eighteen experienced bullying nationwide (National Center for Education Statistics, 2019).	• An estimated 10 to 20 percent of Canadian youths are affected by a mental illness or disorder—the single most disabling group of disorders worldwide.
• Twenty-five percent of teenagers have experienced repeated bullying via cell phone or the internet (GuardChild, n.d.).	• Approximately 5 percent of male youths and 12 percent of female youths aged twelve to nineteen have experienced a major depressive episode.
• Eighty percent of children with a diagnosable anxiety disorder are not getting treatment (Child Mind Institute, 2018).	• The total number of twelve- to nineteen-year-olds at risk of developing depression is a staggering 3.2 million.
• One in three of all adolescents ages thirteen to eighteen will experience an anxiety disorder (Merikangas et al., 2010).	• Only 20 percent of children who need mental health services receive them. (All statistics from Canadian Mental Health Association, 2021)

Figure I.2: Mental health and wellness and the real world of students.

These realities—bullying, mental illness, anxiety—can lead to drug and alcohol abuse, family strife, and school dropouts. Given these realities in the world of students, the assertion that students will be taught about the real world through coercion using the gradebook is, at best, misguided. What if the use of the gradebook for behavioral compliance isn't absolute, as some educators believe it to be? What if there is another way? What if there is an alternative pathway in *teaching* responsibility without punitive grading practices—a better way to hold students accountable?

Conceptually, most (if not all) educators will agree about the need to teach students to be more accountable. Disagreement emerges on the *how*, the processes and practices for doing so. This book is about shifting educators' mindset from *reactively* distorting academic achievement grades when students fall short to *proactively* teaching students to be more accountable for their behavior.

A Shift in Mindset

This shift in mindset from reactive to proactive is anchored in two big ideas. First, schools should teach, develop, nurture, and reinforce positive behavioral attributes (such as respect, responsibility, work ethic, and self-directedness) and student accountability for these attributes as they do academic skills. Second, schools can shift their mindset to teaching, developing, nurturing, and reinforcing positive behavioral attributes by taking advantage of the strength of three processes: (1) sound assessment practices, (2) the Professional Learning Communities at Work® process, and (3) the Response to Intervention (RTI) at Work™ model. These processes will increase the schools' efficiency and effectiveness. Sound assessment practices provide the substance for teaching, assessing, and reporting on the development of positive behavioral attributes. The PLC at Work process provides the culture and a framework of systems, practices, and processes. A three-tier continuum like RTI at Work provides a student-centered perspective that rejects a one-size-fits-all approach.

When schools shift from using punitive and coercive behavioral management practices that use grades as a tool to teaching, developing, nurturing, and reinforcing positive behavioral attributes and student accountability, they are able to prepare students for the real world they will face as adults.

How to Get There

Part I of this book makes the case that a shift in mindset to teach, develop, nurture, and reinforce positive behavioral attributes is strengthened by taking advantage of three processes.

Chapter 1 addresses the first of these processes—sound assessment practices—by highlighting why it is inappropriate and inaccurate to assess student attributes as part of the academic achievement grade. The separation of academic achievement from student attributes is paramount to ensuring the accuracy of any assessment, whether academic or behavioral.

Chapter 2 addresses the role of the PLC at Work process and explores how schools can take advantage of the practices and processes already in place within a professional learning community (PLC) to create a purposeful approach to teaching responsibility. The systematic approach already established in PLCs for identifying goals, assessing those goals, and determining inventions and extensions presents a significant advantage when used to redefine student accountability.

Chapter 3 examines the RTI at Work model and illustrates how a tiered approach to teaching responsibility is not only advantageous but also necessary to maximize the impact on all learners. Educators instinctively know *one size never fits all* so understanding how to layer instruction and intervention is a crucial part of not only establishing a proactive school culture, but achieving meaningful outcomes for those students requiring the most intensive support.

These processes are perfectly aligned to maximize the effectiveness and efficiency of redefining student accountability. While additional practices and processes will be put in place, no major add-on is needed if schools have invested in these three processes.

The chapters in part II provide a comprehensive blueprint for how schools can purposefully create a culture where behavioral attributes receive the instructional attention they deserve. Chapter 4 explores the importance of explicit instruction, assessment, and feedback. The desire for students to be more responsible should be backed by a purposeful effort to teach and reinforce it, rather than resorting to traditional methods of reacting to irresponsibility with consequences. Specifically, the chapter addresses how schools can reimagine a more culturally responsive and expansive norm of what it means to *act appropriately* in school.

In chapter 5, the focus shifts to those inevitable missteps. Despite explicit instruction, there will still be some students who fall short of the established expectations. Specifically, the focus is on how schools can reimagine discipline from being something adults do *to* students to something students *become* characteristically (to become disciplined).

Chapter 6 emphasizes the importance of raising the profile of the development of student attributes, such as responsibility. Working with established norms and routines (such as reporting systems) can signal to both students and families that responsibility and other attributes also matter. What educators give their attention to is what students will eventually believe is important.

In chapter 7, schools transfer the responsibility for monitoring social competence from teachers to students so that students will be able to self-regulate through a process of goal setting, self-monitoring, and self-reflection.

Each chapter ends with questions for learning teams that leaders and teachers can use to reflect on their practices and their schools.

From Informal to Formal

Most schools make an effort to develop students' behavioral attributes. Even if the effort is somewhat haphazard, it is usually moderately effective. Schools do not need to invent something new. Rather, schools must take what was once informal and make it formal, take what has often been hidden and bring it to light. Most educators and parents agree that students need to develop both academic skills and behavioral and social skills to be successful in their adult lives; disagreement concerns how to get there. This book provides a *how* that will leave no doubt about the importance of teaching students to help them become both intellectually and behaviorally competent independent of the gradebook. Using the threat of a low score (or the promise of a high score) to coerce behavioral compliance may produce fear-based, short-term, teacher-controlled compliance, but that may come at the cost of students becoming more self-regulatory where their monitoring, corrections, feedback, and sustainability are internally sourced.

Part I:

A Shift in Mindset

CHAPTER 1

Redefining Student Accountability Within the Assessment Context

Student behavior matters, and it matters so much that we should not conflate behavior with academic performance.

— **DOUGLAS REEVES**

The use of assessment to hold students accountable for behavioral missteps—or the threat of a lower score as a result of certain mistakes—is so much a part of schooling that it isn't questioned and is even encouraged. The onset of curricular standards and the subsequent pivot to criterion-referenced assessment should have put an end to the antiquated practice. However, the tension between having accurate assessments and influencing student behavior remains a significant hurdle schools must overcome. If they overcome it, they can ensure that grades (in whatever form they may take) are a reflection of student learning, not a hodgepodge of the degree to which students met the intended learning goals and how well behaved and responsible they were (Brookhart, 2013).

The Big Ideas

Research does not support that including behavioral missteps with assessment evidence (whether in a single sample of student learning or an overall grade) is best practice. This practice distorts assessment evidence. Punitive grading practices, such as zeros and late penalties, are neither effective instructional strategies nor universal motivators (Guskey, 2015). While teachers may say they do not intend to be punitive, the practices themselves tell another story; reducing assessment scores as a direct result of behavioral missteps *is* punitive.

Traditional practices like punitive grading become entrenched when we educators rely on our philosophies instead of research. Research allows us to justify decisions by saying, "The research indicates that [insert topic] is the most favorable course of action." When we don't have research to support our view, the assertion shifts to "It's my philosophy that [insert topic] is the most favorable course of action." This is being research based when it's convenient, and philosophy is not enough to justify continued use of educational strategies. Consider what the research says schools and educators should prioritize when it comes to assessment.

Prioritize Sound Assessment Practices

Grading is assessment; it is using assessment evidence for summative purposes. The research on sound assessment practices (formative and summative assessment, assessment design, effective feedback, self-assessment, sound grading practices) has been robust since education's renaissance of assessment practices during the late 1990s. The backdrop of the standards movement brought assessment back into focus as essential to ensuring students reach the full depth and breadth of the intended learning. As Paul Black (2013) writes, "Assessment is merely a means to gather evidence about learning. It is the use of the evidence that distinguishes the formative from the summative" (p. 170).

Prioritize Hope, Efficacy, and Achievement

As my colleagues Cassandra Erkens and Nicole Dimich and I write in *Essential Assessment: Six Tenets for Bringing Hope, Efficacy, and Achievement to the Classroom* (Erkens, Schimmer, & Dimich, 2017), "Hope, efficacy, and achievement must remain at the forefront of our classroom assessment practices" (p. 17). While achievement has always been an integral part of assessment and grading, educators sometimes lose sight of the big picture and become too procedural. Grading is not a solely clinical exercise in number crunching; there is a human being on the other end of our grading practices and procedures who must remain in our view, so we educators should be attentive to the emotional side of grading.

Without *hope*—the feeling of positive expectation about a desirable outcome—students are preemptively defeated. Without *efficacy*—the ability to produce that desirable outcome—hope devolves into wishful thinking. At all times, even when they academically or behaviorally stumble, students must be able to envision success and believe that they either can produce that success currently or can cultivate it through a combination of teacher support and personal resolve. When our assessment and grading practices serve to undermine hope or efficacy (or both), we've lost the plot. This is where we can inadvertently send mixed messages to students. On the one hand, we make a concerted effort to build strong relationships that let students know we care about their well-being. On the other hand, we undermine those relationships within the sphere of what truly matters—their learning. Every assessment, whether used formatively or summatively, puts learners in a vulnerable position; to undermine their hope and efficacy through assessment practices is, at best, hypocritical.

In *Performing Under Pressure: The Science of Doing Your Best When It Matters Most*, Hendrie Weisinger and J. P. Pawliw-Fry (2015) reveal that those who best handle pressure approach pressure situations with a *COTE of armor*: "confidence, optimism, tenacity, and enthusiasm" (p. 7). According to Weisinger and Pawliw-Fry (2015), no one performs better with pressure than they do without it. Weisinger and Pawliw-Fry (2015) assert that since pressure in life is unavoidable, the key is to understand how to handle our reactions to pressure. We must understand how pressure affects us, how pressure potentially puts us at risk, and how we can manage pressure moments. Those professional athletes whom we refer to as *clutch* do not actually rise to the occasion; rather, they just don't drop as far as others. They simply manage pressure moments better than others do, thereby creating the illusion that they have risen. For students, assessment, especially when it comes to evidence that's used to determine grades, is as pressure packed as anything they experience.

For many students, the social circumstances of school might be more pressure packed than assessment is, but assessment is *up there* in terms of pressure (whether that pressure is self-inflicted or externally sourced). While it's easy to romanticize the pressure students experience in school as a kind of seasoning for their future, pressure has a devastating impact on performance, which is likely to be magnified for students who have yet to reach full adulthood. Weisinger and Pawliw-Fry (2015) assert the following about pressure.

- It negatively impacts cognitive success; we don't think clearly under pressure.
- It lowers our behavioral skills; our psychomotor skills are compromised.
- It causes us to perform below our capabilities.

- It is often camouflaged within pressure traps; tools such as incentives intensify pressure.

- It is more present in our daily lives than it has ever been before; today's fast-paced world makes pressure unavoidable.

All of this means we educators would be wise to consider the degree to which our grading practices serve to build or undermine our students' COTEs of armor.

Additionally, the competencies of *social-emotional learning* (SEL)—the process through which students regulate emotions, set goals, demonstrate empathy, build healthy relationships, and make constructive choices (Collaborative for Academic, Social, and Emotional Learning [CASEL], n.d.a)—are crucial to consider as schools contemplate the impact of their assessment systems. SEL competencies are exponentially more challenging for students to develop when traditional grading practices leave students with, at best, an opaque view of their achievement and self. The disconnect between the students' self-perceptions and their academic achievement results makes accurate self-observation much more difficult as students consider whether an unfavorable outcome is the result of limited understanding or a behavioral misstep.

Prioritize Accuracy

While grading is not solely clinical, it does have a clinical side that must align with the principles of sound assessment—that is sound measurement. Again, personal or institutional philosophy must take a back seat to the assessment fundamentals that ensure report card grades accurately reflect student learning; grades must be reflections of learning and not commodities that students acquire through the harvesting of points. If grading practices aren't reliable, teachers face challenges with validly interpreting the results.

We often speak of *validity* and *reliability* in that order, but operationally, they work in reverse. Only reliable assessments can allow people to make valid interpretations of the results. As Jay Parkes (2013) writes in the *SAGE Handbook of Research on Classroom Assessment*, "Essentially, the measurement principle of reliability expresses the consistency of examinees or raters across measurement occasions" (p. 107). Parkes identifies three fundamental underpinnings to how reliability is perceived and how it might evolve.

1. **Replication across multiple instances:** The degree of reliability among assessors is determined by multiple tasks assessed by multiple raters across multiple assessment times.

2. **Sampling of observations in a purely statistical sense:** The sampling of student performance allows for generalizable conclusions.

3. **Unidimensionality:** The assessment measures only what it is intended to measure.

The absence or limitation of any of these underpinnings compromises reliability among assessors. In other words, if assessment results aren't replicable, don't provide enough evidence (adequate sampling), or fail to account for confounding factors, the accurate interpretation of assessment results is compromised. Reliability refers to how consistently an assessment measures what it is intended to measure. If an assessment is reliable, its results should be repeatable (Heritage, 2021).

There is debate in the academic literature about the degree to which reliability can be achieved at the classroom level. Some argue that reliability is a prerequisite to validity (Brennan, 1998) while others argue that educators should have some tolerance for unreliability (Kane, 2011) because reliability matters most when the stakes are highest. The balance for teachers is best established when they prioritize reliability through establishing and practicing success criteria and accepting that true, clinical consistency may never be fully achieved; it is not an all-or-nothing endeavor. Research aside, common sense dictates that multiple teachers teaching the same grade-level subject should strive to agree on what excellence looks like and subsequently determine (and report) levels of performance in a like-minded manner.

Once we educators have reliable measures, we can make a *valid* interpretation of the results. Again, teachers must find the balance between the traditional psychometric theory of validity and the social-constructivist view of validity—the tensions between test scores and the values derived from test stakeholders (Bonner, 2013). Educational assessment expert Sarah M. Bonner (2013) suggests common ground can be found in the acceptance of two aspects that constitute appropriate interpretations of assessment evidence: (1) justification and (2) evidence quality.

Teachers striving for validity must also keep in mind that grades do not exist in a vacuum; grades are used for consequential decision making both inside the school (such as for determining interventions) and outside the school (such as for considering university applications). Accurately interpreting assessment results matters.

Connecting Assessment to Student Behavioral Accountability

Schools need to teach, monitor (by both students and teachers), reinforce, assess, and report on student behavioral accountability; however, they must do so separately from academic achievement. This approach needs to be proactive, instructional, and viewed as a top priority by school personnel, students, and parents and families.

Be Proactive

Interestingly, the separation of behavioral attributes from academic achievement is often met with the (false) assertion that this diminishes the importance of those behavioral attributes; the opposite is true. What adults give their attention to is what students believe is important, so through the separation of academics and behavior in schools, we have the potential to increase the profile and importance of developing the whole person. A necessary first step in being proactive is to decide that behavioral attributes matter and that we, collectively and individually, are willing to dedicate the necessary time and resources to develop them in our students. After all, we can't say, "These attributes are just as important as academic learning," but then allocate very little or no time and effort toward helping students with that learning.

A second step in being proactive with behavioral attributes is planning ahead. It might not seem so, but reacting always takes more time than being proactive. Purposefully focusing on establishing positive social norms is more efficient and effective than reacting to students acting inappropriately. We must look at the context within which behaviors occur because this context influences how those behaviors manifest in the first place. It is understandable that some teachers might want to hedge on the unknowable future; we don't know which antisocial behaviors (those that violate social norms) we might experience from students, so why take valuable instructional time handling hypothetical circumstances that typically involve a small percentage of the student population? As tempting as that might seem in the short term, the unpredictable nature of that approach creates an inefficiency for teachers, as they will be interrupted at inopportune times and have to deal with acute situations that could have been prevented. If a behavior is predictable, then it's preventable, so schools can, for the most part, predict and plan for the behavioral missteps that most students will display.

Take an Instructional Approach

Learning social skills is a subset of SEL (Davies & Cooper, 2013). The goal is for students to be SEL competent, which, according to education professors Stephen N. Elliott, Jennifer R. Frey, and Michael Davies (2015), includes being able to acquire "the core competencies necessary to recognize and manage emotions, to set and achieve positive goals, to appreciate the perspectives of others, to establish and maintain positive relationships, to make responsible decisions, and to handle interpersonal situations constructively" (p. 301). However, not all students are ready to jump straight to managing themselves, their emotions, and their relationships. Social and emotional competence will emerge from the development of specific social skills, which are a set of behaviors that initiate and maintain a student's continual adaptation to both the social environment and the rigors of learning (Gresham, 2002).

Educators can and should teach social skills directly. It is, at best, naive to assume students possess the social skills to seamlessly navigate the school experience, so the process for getting students to the goal of SEL independence must be intentional. For student accountability, the focus is precisely on teaching students the social skills that are *academic enablers*—those nonacademic behaviors that elevate the students' opportunities for success (Elliott et al., 2015).

What is curious is how responses to academic missteps and responses to behavioral missteps typically contrast. The response to an academic misstep is always instructional; when students fall short of reaching the intended learning goals, teachers respond with more instruction. However, when students fall short behaviorally, the traditional response has been consequences. It is wise to remember that social skills are academic enablers. The separation of student social skills from academic achievement should result in a parallel instructional mindset.

Be Guided by the Grading True North

Redefining student accountability is an essential aspect of developing a standards-based mindset. Teachers can reimagine the culture of grading and reporting in their classrooms by redefining what grades are and what they are intended to communicate (Schimmer, 2016). By redefining student accountability, repurposing homework, and giving students full credit for their learning, teachers can independently reshape the culture of grading. That reshaping begins with auditing all existing practices through the lens of the *grading true north*: the pairing of accuracy and confidence. That is, all grading practices must pass the following accuracy and confidence tests, or else they must be discontinued.

1. Does the grading practice maintain or increase the accuracy of what is ultimately reported about student achievement?

2. Will students remain confident about their eventual success after experiencing that grading practice?

Through the true north, it's easy to see which grading practices should continue, which need to be adjusted, and which need to immediately stop. Accuracy is the non-negotiable of grading and reporting practices. As Susan M. Brookhart (2013) writes, "Validity is in question when the construct to be measured is not purely achievement but rather some mix of achievement and nonachievement factors" (p. 260). Weisinger and Pawliw-Fry's (2015) COTE of armor places confidence at the forefront of handling any pressure situations, which would include assessment.

It is through this true north process that teachers can self-assess and reveal where accountability for behavioral missteps is inadvertently (or intentionally) influencing achievement decisions. Answer *yes* to both true north questions, and those grading practices should continue. Answer *yes* to only one, and adjustments must be made; we can't have confidence-building grading practices that distort achievement levels, nor can we have accurate grading practices that undermine student confidence. A *no* to both questions means that the grading practices must immediately stop. This process will clarify which grading practices remain relevant, and it will reveal where achievement is being distorted by behavioral attributes.

Assessing Student Responsibility

The most crucial time for any school in redefining student accountability is after the decision to separate academic achievement from behavioral competence is made; the separation of the two must not result in the expectation of responsibility or any other behavioral attribute being reduced to an afterthought. Schools must commit to teaching and assessing behavioral attributes separately, using frequency scales, and having developmentally aligned expectations.

Teach and Assess Behavioral Attributes Separately

When teaching anything, including student behavioral attributes, we have a process to follow: establish clear expectations, establish clear criteria aligned with those expectations, allow students the opportunity to authentically demonstrate those expectations, provide continual feedback in areas of growth, and *assess* students periodically to verify that they are, in fact, becoming more responsible. This process is both simple and complex. It's simple because we know what to do; it's complex because dedicating the time, space, and attention necessary to thoroughly teach students what it means to be responsible isn't always easy.

The question regarding student responsibility and other attributes is *when*, not *if*. Teachers and administrators will be forced to dedicate time to addressing all student behaviors; they must decide whether they would rather be proactive, precorrective, strategic, and fair or reactive, redirective, arbitrary, and equal. Being proactive is always more efficient and effective, as there is greater control and predictability within the process and more students are positively impacted.

Schools would also be wise to think about the teaching, monitoring, and feedback of responsibility as a long continuum. The starting point for both individuals and the collective will determine the degree to which students can (and will) self-regulate their responsibility, along with all other behavioral characteristics. In the long run, it is most desirable to have students move from external monitoring to self-management; from frequent monitoring to infrequent monitoring; from tangible reinforcement to social reinforcement; from individual feedback to group-based feedback.

Schools must identify both the individual and collective points of entry for their context. If schools already have high rates of responsibility (and other prosocial behaviors), then they are likely to begin with developing the SEL and self-regulatory skills. If rates of responsibility (and other prosocial behaviors) are relatively low, schools may take a more direct approach to teaching and monitoring to create a more desirable, prosocial context. One size never fits all, and a contextualized approach will bring about more immediate results. We'll explore the proactive-versus-reactive decision as well as the continuum of instruction and monitoring in greater detail in chapter 4 (page 65).

Use Frequency Scales

Most behavioral attributes that schools will be teaching and measuring in students are binary—either students exhibit a characteristic or they do not. Someone can't be *sort of* responsible along a continuum of quality in the way that quality is described for curricular standards. Therefore, when assessing student responsibility, teachers would be best off using a frequency scale to view student responsibility holistically. The individual moments of responsibility may be binary, but they combine to create a bigger picture of responsibility that is scalable. Research indicates that during assessment, a rating scale with a few clearly discernible levels is most reliable (Brookhart & Guskey, 2019), but this research stops short of dictating the exact number of levels. Often, schools will choose the same number of levels they have established for academic achievement. For example, if students are assessed on a scale of four levels of academic achievement (exemplary, proficient, developing, and novice), then they might also be assessed on a scale of four for exhibiting behavioral attributes (consistently, often, sometimes, and rarely). Figure 1.1 (page 18) provides some examples of frequency scales that could be paired with academic scales. (Chapter 6, page 109, provides more information about developing and using frequency scales for behavioral assessment.)

NUMBER OF LEVELS	ACHIEVEMENT	RESPONSIBILITY
5	**5:** Mastery **4:** Exemplary **3:** Proficient **2:** Developing **1:** Novice	**5:** Consistently **4:** Usually **3:** Often **2:** Sometimes **1:** Rarely
4	**4:** Exemplary **3:** Proficient **2:** Developing **1:** Novice	**4:** Consistently **3:** Often **2:** Sometimes **1:** Rarely
3	**3:** Proficient **2:** Developing **1:** Novice	**3:** Consistently **2:** Sometimes **1:** Rarely

Figure 1.1: Achievement and responsibility scales.

Making assessment reliable (consistent from teacher to teacher) requires clear distinctions between levels (Shweta, Bajpal, & Chaturvedi, 2015). It is easy to establish any number of levels; the challenge is to clearly define the levels to establish the differences among them. While having more levels *feels* more precise, the opposite can be true: with more choices comes more potential variability among assessors. Accuracy comes from clarity, and having fewer levels produces no substantive difference in student performance. Students themselves prefer fewer levels by almost a two-to-one ratio (Dixon, 2004). Importantly, not using a scale at all—taking the "I'll know it when I see it" approach or normatively comparing students—creates, at best, an opaque environment within which students are expected to act and learn.

Developmentally Align Expectations

Behavioral expectations must be aligned with student maturity and physiological stages of development. School districts would be wise to establish a continuum through the grade levels to create a big-picture process for how students develop responsibility. K–12 districts have a seamless opportunity to establish a continuum;

other configurations (such as K–8, 6–12, and 9–12) would need interdistrict communication and alignment, which can be challenging if multiple districts feed into another (four K–8 districts feed into one high school district, for example).

At the elementary school level (K–5), the teaching of responsibility might focus on personal integrity. In *The Seven Habits of Highly Effective People: Powerful Lessons in Personal Change*, Stephen R. Covey (1989) offers a brilliant definition of *integrity* and contrasts integrity with honesty: "Honesty is telling the truth—in other words, *conforming our words to reality*. Integrity is *conforming reality to our words*—in other words, keeping promises and fulfilling expectations" (pp. 195–196). Teaching elementary students to keep promises and fulfill expectations establishes a foundation of personal responsibility—that is, "I do what I say I'm going to do." Initially, teachers and principals establish the expectations, but then (as we will discuss in chapter 7, page 127), students can transition to regulating their own responsibility once they are meeting school-based expectations consistently.

At the middle school level (6–8), the expansion of what it means to be responsible likely entails an additional focus on the social context. Because of young adolescents' need for affiliation and belonging, they must have opportunities to form affirming and healthy relationships with peers (Caskey & Anfara, 2014). The attitudes, beliefs, and values that young adolescents develop during this time often remain with them for life (Brighton, 2007). In particular, responsibility not only includes personal integrity but also expands to prioritize responsibility to others, including both peers and adults. Relationships and belonging matter to middle school students, so establishing norms of responsibility to others is foundational.

At the high school level (9–12), a further expansion of responsibility is likely to include the school and societal contexts. Assuming responsibility to oneself (integrity) and others (relationships), the priority moves to establishing what it means to be a responsible citizen both in and out of school. Students could be asked to reflect on the degree to which they contribute to the greater good of the school, how they can become contributing members of society, or what it means to be socially responsible. High school students are clearly closest to transitioning to the adult world (postsecondary education or employment), so beginning to see the bigger picture of the world around them (and their contributions to it) is most relevant. They are not adults, but we can help them understand what thinking like adults means.

The progression through levels in a frequency scale for behavior is not about establishing strict parameters and *only* focusing on one aspect of responsibility. Elementary school students can also grow in their responsibility to others; middle school students can expand their responsibility to the school context and society as a whole. The prioritization is simply about distributing time and effort, as well as setting the necessary foundation. Students who expand beyond the established priorities are celebrated. The point is to establish a continuum so teachers and principals can leverage their minutes in service of the most favorable outcome. The expansion of responsibility beyond the self, others, or the larger context can happen at any age.

The Big Picture

Separating assessment of behavioral attributes from academic achievement is necessary to ensure that all communication about student learning and development is clear. Compounding the complexity of the separation are the curricular standards that are behavioral in nature, such as standard 4 of SHAPE America's (2013) National Standards for K–12 Physical Education, which states, "The physically literate individual exhibits responsible personal and social behavior that respects self and others." Such standards create another layer of decision making.

Understand That Behavioral Skills Matter

Grades will get students into college, but students' habits and attributes are why they will graduate from college. In fact, it could be argued that student behavioral attributes are more important than academic learning; students find success after high school because they have developed the right habits and dispositions. Students, families, and outside stakeholders may never see successful development of necessary behavioral characteristics as on par with academic achievement; however, they all need to view behavioral characteristics as important and acknowledge that these characteristics matter. According to the Conference Board of Canada (2022), an independent applied-research organization, employability in the 21st century centers on four big ideas: (1) fundamental skills, (2) social and emotional skills, (3) personal-management skills, and (4) teamwork skills. While the fundamental-skills list leans heavily toward academic achievement, the other three align with the idea of teaching, developing, and assessing student behavioral attributes. Figure 1.2 lists the identified social-emotional, personal management, and teamwork skills.

As educators, we must ensure that there is no misunderstanding in our communication to students, parents, and all other stakeholders. Ensuring this requires the following two things to be true: (1) academic achievement grades communicate, without distortion, the degree to which students have met the curricular standards, and (2) important behavioral characteristics and dispositions are taught and developed separately from academics.

SOCIAL AND EMOTIONAL SKILLS

*The skills that describe how you connect with others,
build relationships, solve problems, and interact with people,
whether family, friends, classmates, or coworkers
(Often called soft skills, human skills, or people skills)*

- Active listening
- Resilience
- Working together
- Flexibility

PERSONAL-MANAGEMENT SKILLS

*The personal skills, attitudes, and behaviors that drive
one's potential for growth*

You will be able to offer yourself greater possibilities for achievement when you can:
- Demonstrate positive attitudes and behaviors
- Be responsible
- Be adaptable
- Learn continuously
- Work safely

TEAMWORK SKILLS

The skills and attributes needed to contribute productively

You will be better prepared to add value to the outcomes of a task, project, or team when you can:
- Work with others
- Participate in projects and tasks

Source: Conference Board of Canada, 2022.

Figure 1.2: The Conference Board of Canada employability skills.

Keep Behavioral Instruction Simple

Students, teachers, and even administrators can find themselves referring to pages and pages of rules and regulations that spell out all that students can't do; the educationese within these documents, while superficially impressive, can create more confusion and loopholes than the documents are worth. Chapter 3 (page 45) and chapter 4 (page 65) provide the details of identifying the specific attributes that become the instructional focus, but the point from an assessment perspective is to limit the number of attributes and keep the characteristics simple and overarching.

There are behavioral expectations and attributes that are necessary for specific classroom situations (for example, safety protocols in an automotive class); classroom teachers will individually teach, redirect, reinforce, and follow-up on those. The few universally applicable behavioral attributes, like responsibility, respect, self-directedness, and work ethic, create a ubiquitous focus for the entire faculty. Specific classroom expectations can even branch off the overarching schoolwide ones, creating opportunities for contextualization and continuity. Identifying a few positively stated characteristics makes the characteristics memorable and represents the first step toward efficient and effective establishment of schoolwide social norms and expectations (Horner, Sugai, & Anderson, 2010).

Design Culturally Expansive Social Norms

Accountability, and all social norms and expectations for that matter, also has to be redefined and re-examined through the lens of cultural relevance and inclusivity. It's important to be conscious of the reality that what educators (and society) often think of, by default, as *good, prosocial behavior* has been defined through a narrow cultural lens. What is misunderstood as *misbehavior* in one culture might be considered expected behavior in another. Muhammad Khalifa (2018), author of *Culturally Responsive School Leadership*, asserts that misbehavior is socially constructed within a school (or any context) and that it is critical for schools, especially school leaders, to include parents and other community members in the process of establishing consensus prosocial norms. Chapter 3 (page 45) outlines steps for establishing norms, including ensuring cultural relevance; for now, the separation of academic achievement from behavioral characteristics has to include a conversation about cultural relevance.

Beverly Daniel Tatum (2017), author of *Why Are All the Black Kids Sitting Together in the Cafeteria?*, asserts that educators have increasing awareness of "the central importance of the development of a group identity among of youth of color" (p. 134). She posits that if the dominant messages that most children of color receive (either subliminally or overtly) disproportionately favor White identity and norms, then their own cultural identity will be diminished. Tatum (2017) writes:

> From early childhood through the preadolescent years, Black children are exposed to and absorb many of the beliefs and values of the dominant White culture, including the idea that Whites are the preferred group in U.S. society. The stereotypes, omissions, and distortions that reinforce notions of White superiority are breathed in by Black children as well as White. Simply as a function of being socialized in a Eurocentric culture, some Black children may begin to value the role models, the lifestyles, and images of beauty represented by the dominant group more highly than those of their own cultural group. (p. 134)

Tatum (2017) adds that positive cultural images and messages are how to counter this tilted message, and although she writes specifically from the Black perspective, it is reasonable to apply these assertions to all cultures represented in schools. Countering the traditional messages of *good behavior* in schools is necessary to create authentic, culturally relevant spaces.

Acknowledge Behavioral Academic Standards

Some subjects have curricular standards that are behavioral in nature. This presents a dilemma that schools must resolve to establish a clear boundary between those behaviors that influence the achievement grade and those that represent a behavioral misstep or a code-of-conduct violation. For example, standard 4 of SHAPE America's (2013) National Standards for K–12 Physical Education declares, "The physically literate individual exhibits responsible personal and social behavior that respects self and others." On the surface, this looks like a contradiction; schools work to separate academic achievement from behavioral characteristics, yet the standards are behavioral in nature. Physical education is not alone. The National Core Arts Standards, for example, include, "Cooperate as a creative team to make interpretive choices for a drama/theatre work" (HS; National Coalition for Core Arts Standards, 2014). *Cooperation* and *responsible personal and social behaviors* are two examples of the dilemma that teachers must reconcile when drawing the line between achievement grades and social competence.

A simple way to reconcile this dilemma is to identify the behaviors that, if chronic or severe, would result in a discipline referral to administration. Those behaviors should be expected but should not be included in any grade determination to avoid a kind of double dipping unique to a few subjects. For example, physical education students who exhibit poor conduct or act as selfish teammates are clearly not being personally or socially responsible to others or themselves; however, if this behavior or attitude were to persist, it is unlikely that the teacher would refer the students to administration for a code-of-conduct violation. Therefore, this type of behavior belongs in an achievement grade because it is an identified learning goal. On the other hand, students who show physical aggression toward an opponent that results in risky or dangerous behavior (such as shoving the student into the back wall of the gymnasium) violate the school's code of conduct. This is unacceptable in any classroom situation and should not be included in grade determination. Instead, it should be handled through the school conduct policy. The existence of standards that are behavioral in nature should not open the floodgates to allow all behavioral missteps to influence achievement decisions.

The process for deciding whether a behavioral misstep should be included in an academic achievement grade begins with determining whether the behavioral misstep is relatively particular to the subject; it need not be exclusive but it should be rare. Figure 1.3 provides a simple decision-making flowchart teachers can follow to make this determination.

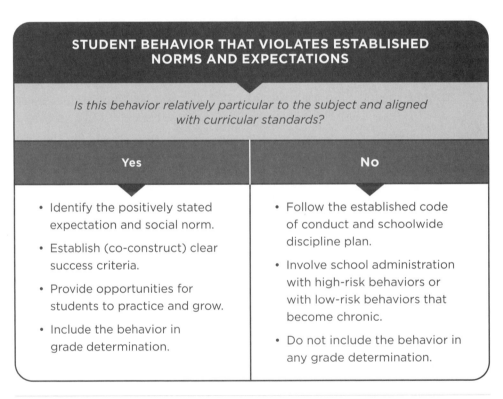

Figure 1.3: Flowchart for deciding which behavioral missteps should be included in academic grade determination.

*Visit **go.SolutionTree.com/behavior** to download a free reproducible version of this figure.*

Behavioral standards belong in achievement grades, but that does not mean teachers can openly incorporate all student behaviors. Behavioral standards must be contextualized, the criteria for meeting those standards must be specified, and the process for responding must be clarified. Using the simple flowchart in figure 1.3 will nudge this process forward.

Summary

Through the promise or threat of the grade, teachers employing traditional assessment and grading practices have managed student behavior through the gradebook. Reshaping the assessment and grading paradigm is overdue; it's time that building hope and efficacy replaced leveraging behavioral compliance as a primary outcome of the assessment process. Accuracy in reporting student achievement matters, which means all nonachievement factors, like responsibility, must be handled separately from the achievement grade.

Teaching is proactive, purposeful, and positively focused on the desirable outcomes; teaching means helping students develop in themselves that which they do not currently have. Some educators may believe they are teaching students life lessons through the application of aversive consequences, but that's not teaching. When accurate assessment is paired with confidence, teachers have a metaphorical compass to decide which grading practices lead to more effective and efficient communication of acquired skills. This true north is the foundation on which teachers can begin to reshape the culture of grading in their classrooms.

The assessment of students' behavioral characteristics is necessary since we can't develop anything or anyone without assessment; coaches can't develop their athletes without assessing them. These important characteristics can't only be important when student missteps emerge or when adults are annoyed. K–12 schools and school districts have the opportunity to create a longitudinal continuum of development through which students apply behavioral attributes first to themselves and then to others, to the school context, and to the world around them.

What adults (including teachers) pay attention to is what students eventually believe is important. The conversation about what's important and the lens through which that determination is made must be culturally expansive to achieve real equity in schools. The narrow view of good behavior has to be dismantled and replaced with a breadth of inclusivity that levels the cultural playing field and accounts for varied actions. Keep behavioral instruction simple, keep it universal, and keep it focused on those characteristics we know will benefit our students long term in any context.

Questions for Learning Teams

1. What quotation or passage encapsulates your main takeaway from this chapter? What immediate action (small, medium, or large) will you take as a result of this takeaway? Explain both to your team.

2. Is it will or skill that more prevents you or your colleagues from separating academic achievement from responsibility (and other behavioral attributes)? What needs to be done to increase the will or skill?

3. Why are academic missteps traditionally met with instruction while behavioral missteps are met with consequences? Why is an instructional response to behavioral missteps challenging to implement?

4. What existing procedures or systems in your school (or district) could be utilized to hold students accountable without distorting their achievement levels?

5. How have behavioral standards been incorporated into student achievement grades? Do you foresee any adjustments to current practice? Explain why or why not.

6. Do working definitions of *good behavior* in your school (or district) hold up under the scrutiny of a culturally responsive and expansive lens? What needs to be done to rectify any inconsistencies?

CHAPTER 2

Redefining Student Accountability Within the PLC at Work Context

Educators who are building a professional learning community recognize that they must work together to achieve their collective purpose of learning for all. Therefore, they create structures to promote a collaborative culture.

—RICHARD DUFOUR

As educators, we should aim for learning for all, and not just academic learning. We must also prioritize the learning of behavioral attributes. Learning for all, however, is easier said than accomplished. What we have come to collectively know is that the complexities of teaching make working collaboratively the most effective way to reach this goal; however, the existence of collaboration alone is insufficient. Collaborative teams need a purposeful process and definitive actions to make efficient use of their collaborative time. The irony within most professions, including education, is that meetings are both loathed and necessary. Therefore, when collaborating, we must make the most of this time by implementing protocols that will maximize collaborative practices' impact on student learning.

Schools that operate as professional learning communities have an inherent advantage when it comes to redefining student accountability since the *redefining* must be a collective effort. Teachers, students, and the community must be aligned in their vision of student accountability; teachers and administrators will primarily be responsible for creating the school culture within which students develop their responsible habits and dispositions. Rather than seeing the effort surrounding student responsibility as yet another initiative, schools can take advantage of the established norms of the PLC at Work process to infuse this effort into the larger context of learning—both academically and socially—for all.

The Big Ideas

Globally, PLC concepts have been implemented across a variety of settings. Some schools and districts have freely applied the PLC label to any collaborative efforts, leaving educators without a final, universal agreement on the characteristics of a PLC (Lomos, 2017; Sleegers, den Brok, Verbiest, Moolenaar, & Daly, 2013; Vescio, Ross, & Adams, 2008). According to University of Florida School of Teaching and Learning professors Vicki Vescio, Dorene Ross, and Alyson Adams (2008), the members of a PLC "must be able to articulate their outcomes in terms of data that indicate changed teaching practices and improved student learning" (p. 82). That means student accountability within the PLC process must result in teachers' becoming more competent at creating the necessary conditions for students to learn to be more personally responsible.

Why PLC?

There's nothing preventing teachers from redefining student accountability on their own; there's nothing preventing a school from doing the same in absence of the PLC process. The question, though, is not *Can they?* but *Should they?* The inconsistent processes through which individual teachers would respond to irresponsible behavior without a unifying protocol has the potential to make things worse. A challenge schools face is that while teachers expect academic missteps and reconcile them through instructional interventions, teachers often view behavioral missteps as disruptions and meet these missteps with aversive consequences. The vast majority of teachers' frustration stems from the fact that training on how to respond to antisocial behavior is far less common than training on responding to academic mistakes. So, if schools need to improve teacher practice and student learning when it comes to accountability, the PLC model is perfect for both.

A professional learning community is just that: a community where the professionals learn. This means that growth in both individual capacity and organizational capacity is essential. Building capacity is the key to the sustainability of PLCs (Hargreaves & Fink, 2006). Teachers' limited capacity and relative discomfort in teaching, developing, and assessing student accountability make approaching this effort through the PLC model wise. Collaboration alone, however, is not enough to improve teacher capacity. Schools must focus on the right work (DuFour, 2011), making collaboration the *means*, not the *end*. The collaborative efforts must be professionally focused on expanding all team members' capacity for redefining student accountability. Without that clarifying structure and focus, collaborative team meetings could easily devolve into a voicing of grievances about how irresponsible students are.

The key shift within a PLC is the focus on student learning. An expansion of teacher capacity is incomplete if it doesn't lead to improved student performance; what's most important is not whether teachers taught something but whether students learned it. The research has unequivocally shown that student learning increases when teachers participate in the PLC process (Bolam, McMahon, Stoll, Thomas, & Wallace, 2005; DuFour & Reeves, 2016; Paterson, 2019; Vescio et al., 2008). Participation in a PLC leads teachers to hold themselves and their colleagues more accountable for student failures and deepens their level of commitment to improving student performance through their own professional growth (Moulakdi & Bouchamma, 2020). We want students to become more responsible, and our collective professional growth and refinement of strategies will make that happen.

What Are Structure and Soul?

In the *Canadian Journal of Educational Administration and Policy*, Ray Williams, Ken Brien, Crista Sprague, and Gerald Sullivan (2008) posit that the successful transformation of schools into a PLC is impacted by operational and organizational characteristics. To borrow a phrase from Rosabeth Moss Kanter (2004), these characteristics provide the *structure* and the *soul* of a PLC; though Kanter was referring to the role of a leader in shaping both structural changes and emotional aspects of change, the reference is still apropos.

The *operational characteristics* provide the structure. Establishing essential operational habits such as professional learning, data-based decision making, and the building of systemic trust are what Williams and colleagues (2008) believe are necessary to maximize the impact of a PLC. Professional learning is embedded within daily collaborative work as teachers collectively gain, share, and implement their learning to create a continuous cycle (Hargreaves & Fullan, 2012; Richmond & Manokore, 2011). While the embedded professional learning can take on various formats, it is always focused on individual and collective growth.

Data-based decision making means we educators have developed a habit of using reliable and actionable information to determine instructional interventions and extensions; this would disproportionately result in the use of common formative assessment to both engineer the professional dialogue and make appropriate instructional maneuvers (Erkens, 2016). Systemic trust is the backbone of a PLC (Hargreaves, 2007) and grows organically as teachers build collaborative relationships that are reciprocally dependent and fiercely student centered.

When we build a culture of trust, use reliable information to make clearheaded decisions, and commit to ongoing professional learning, our collective efficacy (our belief in our collective ability to positively impact student learning) expands through the structural norms that refresh the assertion, "This is how we do business."

The *organizational characteristics*—school culture, distributed leadership, and capacity building—provide the soul. These characteristics begin with the establishment of a positive school culture. A school's culture influences people's readiness for change (Antinluoma, Ilomäki, Lahti-Nuuttila, & Toom, 2018), and collaborative cultures are effective and positively influence student achievement (Fullan, 2015; Stoll, Bolam, & Greenwood, 2007). Leadership also provides a piece of the soul since principals have a disproportionate influence on the professional climate and activities of all within the school. Principals act as links among all the teachers, the work of the collaborative teams, and the schoolwide efforts to increase achievement for all students; their opportunities to see the big picture are fundamental.

However, leadership is dynamic and can be distributed to many individuals who lead collaborative conversations about improving student learning and professional practice; it's a symbiotic relationship. Distributed leadership thrives when strong formal leadership defines the professional autonomy and authority of informal leaders, secures professional learning resources and opportunities, models the vision, and works to establish a trusting environment (Harris, 2011).

Capacity building is the third organizational characteristic Williams and colleagues (2008) believe is critical to the successful implementation of a PLC. At the core of the PLC is the *PL*—the *professional learning* of the teachers as individuals and as a collective. Participation in a PLC leads to positive changes in teaching practices (Little, 2011). The social capital, according to Andy Hargreaves and Michael Fullan (2012), is most important, as it accelerates the growth of human capital, deepens trust, and strengthens the quality of the collaborative conversations.

The structure (operational characteristics) and the soul (organizational characteristics) of a PLC provide a framework and the disposition that establish a balance between the clinical and the affective aspects of teaching. Structure without soul is procedure without humanity; soul without structure is humanity without purpose.

Together, they can create the opportunity (structure) for teachers to feel that their actions will have an efficacious impact on student learning (soul).

Why the PLC at Work Process?

Schools implementing the PLC at Work process are in a particularly advantageous position when it comes to redefining student accountability for behavioral attributes. While many PLC models are put forth in education, the PLC at Work process and practices offer optimal clarity as to what the work of a PLC is (improving professional practice), who the work of a PLC is for (students), and how a PLC measures its success (maximized achievement). The systems, structures, practices, and processes that permeate the PLC at Work process first envisioned by Richard DuFour and Robert Eaker (1998) remain the standards by which all other PLC models must be judged. And while the standards and expected learning intentions have increased in sophistication over time, the PLC at Work process remains unwaveringly focused on student learning through three big ideas, six characteristics, and four critical questions. Therefore, the PLC at Work process is specifically endorsed here as the most efficient and effective framework through which schools can redefine student accountability.

The three big ideas of the PLC at Work process keep the spotlight on students; the work of the adults is for the benefit of all learners. First, while a *focus on learning* sounds rudimentary, many of us know and have experienced the ways in which educators can lose focus by fixating on delivery and coverage. The work of the educators is the means. The learning of the students is the end, and that learning must include responsibility and other behavioral characteristics that we know are essential for students to thrive. Second, the work of educators is too complex to operate in isolation, which means effective PLCs build a *collaborative culture*. Professional practice improves when teachers work together to clarify essential student learning, collectively develop common assessments and criteria for that learning, analyze the evidence of that learning to perform instructional maneuvers or determine appropriate interventions, and use that evidence to learn from one another. Third, a *focus on results* means intentions are irrelevant; what matters is the impact at the student level. "I taught it, but they didn't learn it" is replaced by "If they didn't learn it, then we didn't teach it." We may have covered it, but without learning on the back end, there is no teaching on the front end.

The characteristics of a PLC at Work and the redefinition of student accountability seamlessly align, and this alignment is detailed in the next section. While the big ideas create the culture, the day-to-day work of educators emerges through the elements of a PLC that become the way a school operates. The interface with students comes through the four critical questions, which is how schools will take action to redefine accountability with students at the forefront. Systems are developed for us as educators; practices are what we implement with students. The elements of a PLC represent the systems within which the educators operate, while the four critical questions are the practices we implement with students.

PLC at Work and Student Accountability

While the PLC at Work process primarily centers on academic achievement, the seamlessness with which the process can be applied to student accountability makes it most desirable in establishing a collective focus on the whole child. Practically speaking, this means schools need not see the work surrounding student accountability and other behavioral characteristics as an add-on; the existing structures, systems, practices, and processes can function regardless of whether the collaborative conversations are anchored in academic or behavioral achievement. The elements of the PLC at Work process (DuFour, DuFour, Eaker, Many, & Mattos, 2016; described in the following sections) make it perfectly situated to provide the foundational habits through which schools address student accountability.

Shared Mission, Vision, Values, and Goals

Here is where a PLC can expand its definition of student success to include the nonacademic characteristics and behavioral dispositions once thought of as the hidden curriculum. The claim that we teach more than just the curricular standards emerges as merely a platitude when that assertion is not supported with dedicated time in service of that mission and vision.

By sharing in the mission, vision, values, and goals of students' learning responsibility, schools move from *me* to *we*; they move from individual (potentially inconsistent) classroom definitions of responsibility to a shared focus and common understanding of the desirable outcome of their efforts. The clarity that emerges for students is as desirable as the consistency with which teachers refer to the criteria of responsibility. This goes a long way to ensuring that criteria are embedded and automatic.

Collective Inquiry

Before we collaborate, we have to establish *why* we are collaborating. Without first establishing the focus of the work, schools can become distracted in two ways. First, they can inadvertently conflate PLCs and meetings; meetings are certainly part of a PLC, but they do not represent the entirety of the work. Second, schools can lose sight of the *L* in *PLC*—that in a learning community, everyone, including the educators, learns. Establishing collective inquiry as the purpose of the work to explore the mission, vision, values, and goals is at the heart of how educators will grow.

While there are many inquiry models that differ in their minutiae, most follow a cycle of ask, investigate, create, discuss, and reflect. The collective inquiry is driven by a question—for example, What is the most effective and efficient way to help students learn to be more responsible? That question drives a real-time investigation that centers on improved practices that lead students to develop habits of responsibility. The investigation leads to thoughts about appropriate applications and actions, which each member of the collaborative team comes prepared to discuss; the discussion leads to personal reflection about growth in professional practice. This inquiry cycle ensures the process is not reduced to a shortsighted goal where simply getting students to do what they're told is the outcome.

Collaborative Culture

The collaborative culture is the cornerstone of a PLC (DuFour et al., 2016). It is through a collaborative culture that the shared mission, vision, values, and goals are established as the substance of collaborative conversations; we need a purpose for meeting, as collaborating for the sake of collaborating is the fastest way to push teachers back into isolation. Collective inquiry within a collaborative culture is precisely how teacher growth will occur.

Collaboration will center on three aspects of the work. First, the collaboration will focus on establishing clear criteria for what it means for students to be responsible. Teams (or ideally, schools) must interpret student actions consistently. When inferring, which requires professional judgment, teams (or schools) need to engage in calibration to establish alignment among all members. Second, teachers will collaborate on common assessment results. Academically, this is relatively straightforward, as teams will create assessments anchored in the curricular standards. For student responsibility, most discussion will center on what team members have observed and the frequency with which students are meeting the expectations (criteria). Third, the collaboration will be grounded in the appropriate instructional response, from both intervention and extension perspectives.

Action Orientation and Experimentation

Here's where teams are going to try new things; their action and experimentation come from the results of their collective inquiry and collaborative conversations. This is not an arbitrary action but an execution of the hypotheses collectively determined by the teams. Implementing the ideas teams came up with while wondering about promising practices is what will create the conditions for student responsibility to develop.

Some strategies won't work; that's the nature of experimentation and professional growth. Teams have to be comfortable with imperfection, and so do school administrators and district leaders. If school and district leaders don't embrace imperfections and implementation errors, teachers will retreat to what's comfortable rather than experiment their way toward effectiveness. When leaders and teams embrace and support the messiness of change, teachers see implementation errors and missteps as taking them one step closer to competence instead of to incompetence.

Commitment to Continuous Improvement

The secret to an effective PLC is that the journey is the destination; the learning never stops. Teams will experience success but can never settle or feel complete. The gathering and, more importantly, the use of data to fuel continuous improvement are essential. Whether formal or informal, the data gathered are used to constantly affirm, refine, or enhance the hypotheses developed within the collaborative dialogue.

Every school year presents a new cohort of students, and while past successes can remain relevant, past strategies that produced past successes may be ill-suited for some students' situations or dispositions. Schools will be either creating the culture of responsibility, refining the culture of responsibility, or transferring the responsibility through a process of student investment, agency, and self-assessment. Every educator knows that perfection never arrives, so schools must find a balance between the celebration of successes and the drive for continual growth.

Focus on Results

The central question for all PLCs is this: Are our collective actions producing the desired result? That's it. If the answer to the question is *yes*, then the desired result is long-term sustainability that avoids the "blitz approach" when habits and social norms waver. If the answer is *no*, then the necessary instructional adjustments, assessment evidence, interventions, and professional learning have to all be considered in service of the agreed-on mission, vision, values, and goals.

Intents, hopes, wishes, and wonders are simply not good enough when our students' futures are at stake. Claiming to be student centered and actually being student centered are two different mindsets; it's easy to claim to be student centered while remaining rigid in approach, leaving students solely at fault for their lack of success. Students must be actively invested in their development of responsible habits.

When students are not, student-centered educators first look in the mirror and ask, "What could we do differently to bring about more student growth?"

The characteristics of a PLC emerge organically and do not represent a linear checklist. Other than the shared mission, vision, values, and goals, which are likely to be established first, these characteristics can emerge and develop in a variety of ways. Does a fixation on continuous improvement spawn a movement toward collective inquiry that solidifies the collaborative culture, or does the collaborative culture drive a collective inquiry that creates a professional environment of continuous improvement? It doesn't matter. What matters is these characteristics are reflective of teachers' professional experience so that conditions are ripe to maximize both academic achievement and social competence.

Four Critical Student Accountability Questions

While the characteristics in the previous section represent the systems and structures a PLC establishes for educators, the four critical questions of a PLC at Work represent the day-to-day practices that operationalize the mission, vision, values, and goals (DuFour et al., 2016). Again, the point is to seamlessly immerse the redefining of student accountability in the existing structures of the PLC at Work process. Schools can redefine student accountability in the absence of the four critical questions; however, those schools will have the additional task of establishing a process (meaning an add-on) through which they redefine accountability.

Question 1: What Do We Want Students to Know or Be Able to Do?

Collaborative teams in a PLC at Work would typically answer this question by identifying one or more mutually agreed-on priority standards. Through a collaborative process, teams identify those standards that are challenging to teach, important to learn, and also challenging for students to achieve. These criteria for identifying priority standards drive the need for collaborative conversations because collectively, we will be more efficient and effective than if we went about the work in isolation (DuFour et al., 2016).

There is no reason that the answer to this question can't also be *responsibility*. We have to put our attention on that which we claim to be important. If we say that we're about the whole child and that behavioral attributes matter, then we have to take a whole-child approach and not allow this first critical question to be exclusive to the academic domain. Too often, we say we want something but don't match the desire for the optimal outcome with the necessary effort to produce it. The answering of this question sets forth a process for teams to identify what is specifically being developed, what transparent process they will use, and what specific criteria and characteristics will manifest as students become more responsible.

Question 2: How Will We Know That They Know It or Can Do It?

This is the assessment piece that chapter 1 (page 9) focused on. However, unlike academic standards, for which teams will collaboratively design assessments, student responsibility will be assessed through observations and experiences that emerge as students do or don't exhibit the specific habits and actions that embody the criteria for responsible behavior. We can't develop anything without assessing it, but that assessment need not mimic the assessment methods or formats used for academic skills.

The work within the collaborative teams will establish the necessary alignment to ensure reliable inferences about what students are noticing and the various ways students can authentically demonstrate it. The depth and breadth of the assessment literacy discussed in chapter 1 go a long way to securing a clear and consistent assessment process. Collaborative teams are also poised to collect evidence to examine how students are progressing over time, how effective instructional efforts have been to date, and what's next to maintain (or re-establish) a positive growth trajectory for students.

The gathered evidence (data) will be less about numbers and spreadsheets and more about actions and observations. The gathering of evidence is not likely to mirror that of a common formative assessment designed for an acute academic moment. It is instead likely to be a moment when team members collectively examine the accumulated evidence from longitudinal observations and reflections to take inventory of student successes, align collective responses, and recalibrate for another longitudinal period of time.

Assessment is the engine that drives the PLC at Work process. The first two critical questions are assessment questions, and the last two questions are responding-to-assessment-evidence questions. The absence of sound assessment practices and principles will result in an ineffective, inefficient, and inconsistent approach to redefining student accountability.

Question 3: How Will We Respond When Some Students Don't Know It or Can't Do It?

We will explore the intervention side of redefining behavioral accountability in depth in chapter 3 (page 45), but for now, it's important to know that intervention decisions are made within the collaborative team context. The planned, purposeful, and proactive instructional approach to behavioral characteristics leads to collaborative decisions about what interventions are needed, who needs them, how they will be delivered, the degree to which the students will be actively involved, and the necessary information (data) that will reveal the interventions are no longer necessary.

Some teachers face a hurdle in recognizing that using behavioral interventions and taking an instructional approach are how we will establish a new norm of pro-social behaviors; they don't realize that the punishment paradigm doesn't produce a behavioral epiphany. Punitive approaches (like out-of-school suspension) do not reduce or prevent misbehavior (Hannigan, Hannigan, Mattos, & Buffum, 2021). Some students will be acutely responsive to threats of punishment or coercive action, but their responsiveness is the result of external fear rather than internal growth. We can minimize (or even eliminate) this hurdle when the academic intervention process already established within the PLC at Work process is widened to include behavioral interventions that are anchored in further instruction instead of exclusionary practices and shame.

Question 4: How Will We Extend the Learning for Those Who Already Know It or Can Do It?

Regulation of one's own responsibility—the idea that students are responsible in the absence of any adult monitoring—is the ultimate goal. We extend the learning for these students by releasing the assessment process to them through self-assessment opportunities. This allows for more self-determined manifestations of responsible behavior and actions, and even allows for leadership opportunities where these students help guide and support their peers. It is not these students' responsibility to provide support and intervention for their peers identified in the question 3 processes; however, many students thrive in leadership roles, so while this shouldn't be a non-negotiable expectation, it can be an opportunity.

Students may also receive opportunities to show responsibility within the greater community. Local organizations, important social movements, and acute community needs all provide students with opportunities to extend their responsible dispositions and habits to work that impacts the world around them. Again, while we cannot mandate these opportunities, we can make students aware of them.

This helps students see that authentic application of these developed skills exists and that responsibility is not just a "school thing."

A Cycle of Continuous Improvement

The four critical questions provide the framework through which continuous improvement is possible (DuFour et al., 2016). Each collaborative team meeting is focused on one (or more) of the four questions, which ensures that conversations are student centered, growth focused, and professionally relevant. When we talk about what we are going to do to support our students, internal accountability is established, and meetings remain relevant in perpetuity.

A collaborative team becomes distracted when one of the four questions is not the focal point of the collaborative conversations. Teams have other reasons to meet, but it is critical that they not mistake those other meetings for collaborative team time. Collaborative team time focused on the four critical questions must be considered sacred and protected because the professional growth that happens through collective inquiry and collaborative conversations cannot occur through email; discussions about field trips and upcoming special events can.

The Big Picture

Although the list of student attributes that are informally nurtured both in and out of the school setting is long, schools would be wise to emphasize depth over breadth when determining the core of what collaborative teams will formally focus on. Prioritizing the attributes, determining the success criteria, and then collectively determining the appropriate lessons and interventions are how schools will take their efforts to scale. In other words, through consolidation, calibration, and correctives (addressed in chapter 5, page 85), schools will bring the once-hidden curriculum out of the shadows.

Consolidate Student Attributes

Most collaborative teams within a PLC at Work already habitually prioritize academic standards for the purpose of designing common formative assessments used to drive both student learning and professional growth. However, unlike the academic process, behavioral prioritization is best done schoolwide, as having each collaborative team go through this process independently would create more problems and inconsistencies than it would solve. Consistency among the adults will only happen when all faculty members are involved in the initial stages of this identification. The degree to which students can and should be involved in this initial process will be context dependent; ideally, they would be involved, but that involvement might come before (such as with student surveys) or after (if students debrief following the initial teacher discussion). It *could* happen simultaneously, with students joining the teachers, but again, the authenticity of students' feelings of empowerment will depend on the already-established school culture (more on student involvement and self-assessment to come in chapter 7, page 127).

Parallel to the identification of priority academic standards, schools (through a comprehensive and inclusive process) need to establish a small number of behavioral characteristics that will be universal focal points. This big picture should be about universally applicable attributes that all teachers and students, regardless of context, can fully immerse themselves in. Rather than a long list of don'ts, these few universally applicable attributes lend themselves to a depth of instruction, and also will be simpler for students to remember and, eventually, recall at a moment's notice. Again, other attributes will also be taught in finite contexts (like in woodworking or shop class) or in informal ways as they emerge (like with teaching the whole child). But the prioritized attributes will purposefully receive a disproportionate number of instructional minutes.

Larry Ainsworth (2013) suggests four criteria by which academic standards are to be prioritized.

1. **Endurance:** Will proficiency in this standard provide students with the knowledge and skills that will be of value beyond the present?

2. **Leverage:** Does the standard have crossover applications within the content area and for other content areas (that is, interdisciplinary connections)?

3. **Readiness for the next level of learning:** Will proficiency in this standard provide students with the essential knowledge and skills that are necessary for future success?

4. **External exams:** Are the concepts and skills ones that students are most likely to encounter on annual standardized tests, college entrance exams, and occupational competency exams?

The first two—endurance and leverage—will be most essential for schools establishing their small number of schoolwide prioritized attributes. Readiness for the next level would be a district-level consideration as a K–8, 6–12, or K–12 continuum is being established. There is a fine line between present-day readiness and an expectation that prematurely projects students to the next level. For example, students developing into responsible middle schoolers will naturally transition to becoming responsible high schoolers; readiness comes from succeeding today, not from trying to replicate tomorrow's expectations. The *external* piece does not necessarily have to be an exam, of course, but could represent an external application that grows through the K–12 continuum we discussed in chapter 1 (page 9). Rather than reinventing new processes, schools can transfer systems and structures currently operating on the academic side of the ledger to the behavioral side.

Almost every school I've encountered has *respect* and *responsibility* as two of its core attributes. Beyond those, the remaining attributes may be more granular at the elementary level and more global at the secondary level. Figure 2.1 illustrates how the behavioral attributes might evolve through the various levels.

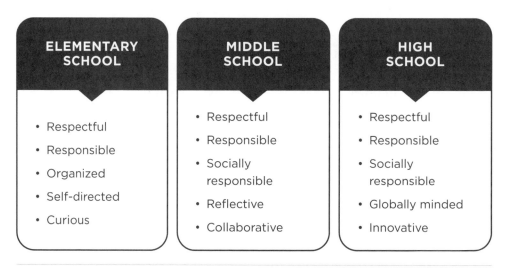

ELEMENTARY SCHOOL

- Respectful
- Responsible
- Organized
- Self-directed
- Curious

MIDDLE SCHOOL

- Respectful
- Responsible
- Socially responsible
- Reflective
- Collaborative

HIGH SCHOOL

- Respectful
- Responsible
- Socially responsible
- Globally minded
- Innovative

Figure 2.1: Examples of student attributes by school level.

If you examine Figure 2.1 through a K–12 lens, you can see how the characteristics expand through the levels. It is not the case that elementary students can't be globally minded or socially responsible; they can. The point is to identify the small number of prioritized attributes that make up the core program of instruction, feedback, self-reflection, and growth.

Calibrate Student Attributes

Another core activity for collaborative teams or even the PLC as a whole is to determine the success criteria for each attribute and then calibrate those criteria to ensure consistency with observations. While some formal assessment could be possible (for example, students could be prompted to write a response to a historical figure's degree of social responsibility), most of the assessment will happen organically through natural day-to-day interactions. Not only does the establishment of criteria build consistency among the adults, but it also makes self-awareness and self-management more possible long term. Again, the degree to which students are involved in this process before, during, or after will be contextually determined.

The assessment of all student attributes will be based on inferences rather than right or wrong answers, so calibration among collaborative teams is essential to ensure expectations are appropriate. Figure 2.2 illustrates a simple example of what the criteria for responsibility could look like.

RESPONSIBILITY

THE STUDENT:

- Is prepared for the day's learning
- Productively and efficiently makes use of class time
- Takes ownership of their actions and behaviors
- Positively contributes to learning activities and the learning environment
- Actively listens and stays on task
- Keeps their workspace clean and organized; cleans up after they're done
- Ignores distractions; makes learning-centered contributions

Figure 2.2: Responsibility success criteria.

Figure 2.2 is not an exhaustive list. There are other ways to demonstrate responsibility; the listed criteria provide students with examples of what the attribute (in this case, responsibility) might look like. Figure 2.2 is also not meant to be *the* singular answer. The examples schools list as criteria should organically emerge from context-specific, culturally responsive norms. The point is to establish criteria that let everyone know what to look for and on what attributes to provide feedback, and to create a foundation of strong personal and collective monitoring within the students themselves.

Summary

Schools operating as PLCs have an inherent advantage when redefining account-ability because the systems, structures, processes, and practices of collaborative teams within a PLC are as seamlessly effective and efficient for responsibility as they are for any academic goal. The structure (operational characteristics) and soul (organizational characteristics) of a PLC provide schools with the predictable and reliable framework needed to create and sustain a long-term approach to teaching responsibility or any other student attribute.

In particular, the PLC at Work process is the most comprehensive model for schools to embed professional learning. The three big ideas of a PLC ensure that educators are focused on student success. The elements of the PLC process present a profile of habitual practices and attitudes that drive the professional learning experience. Accountability will be redefined only when the teachers collectively become curious about how to challenge tradition and take an instructional (rather than punitive) approach when students fall short of expectations.

Day-to-day work must be galvanized around the four critical questions. Generally, collaborative teams become distracted if their meetings do not focus on at least one of the four questions. The questions establish an instructional focus, place assessment at the center of the decision-making process, and have teams intentionally consider both interventions and extensions to support all learners. The four questions are comprehensive, they are process oriented, and they leave little to chance in terms of how all students can learn what responsibility, respectfulness, and any other attributes that enhance long-term success mean.

Questions for Learning Teams

1. What quotation or passage encapsulates your main takeaway from this chapter? What immediate action (small, medium, or large) will you take as a result of this takeaway? Explain both to your team.

2. Which of the operational characteristics (professional learning, data-based decision making, and systemic trust) do you identify as aspects of strength within your school context? Which aspects are in need of strengthening?

3. Which of the organizational characteristics (school culture, distributed leadership, and capacity building) do you identify as aspects of strength within your context? Which aspects are in need of strengthening?

4. To what degree is your school context a collaborative culture focused on collective professional inquiry (focused, somewhat focused, or not focused)? What would it take to establish or strengthen an investigatory approach to redefining student accountability?

5. How comfortable are you with on-the-job experimentation and action research (comfortable, somewhat comfortable, or not comfortable)? Explain. What would make you even more comfortable?

6. Knowing that you and your colleagues are all at different points along the continuum, do you think *skill* or *will* has more greatly inhibited your collective ability to redefine student accountability?

CHAPTER 3

Redefining Student Accountability Within an RTI at Work Context

RTI challenges the basic premises of some educators by assuming that all students can learn, that all educators will take responsibility for all learners, and that schools will adjust their current environments and practices so that this can occur.

—AUSTIN BUFFUM, MIKE MATTOS, AND CHRIS WEBER

While the PLC at Work process provides the framework for redefining student responsibility, RTI at Work provides the model that allows schools to redefine student accountability in a balanced, growth-focused, and student-centered way. The foundation of the RTI at Work continuum is that all learners can be successful if they have instruction, support, and intervention; this is not a one-size-fits-all approach but rather a structure with varying degrees of support and intervention.

The Big Ideas

RTI (response to intervention) typically refers to academic instruction and intervention while PBIS (positive behavioral interventions and supports) refers to behavioral instruction and supports. The synthesis of the two creates a comprehensive approach called *MTSS* (*multitiered system of support*). While differences in focus and implementation may be context dependent, the fundamentals that underpin all three are aligned to create a student-responsive approach to support and inclusion. The focus on RTI throughout this chapter is intended to highlight the overlap between those schools implementing RTI at Work within the PLC at Work process. However, the larger picture is that a three-tiered continuum, regardless of the preferred acronym, would be most favorable for developing a comprehensive approach to teaching behavior outside of the gradebook.

Evidence of Effectiveness

According to John Hattie (2018), the implementation of RTI has an effect size of 1.29. To add some perspective, Hattie (2009) asserts an effect size of 1.0 indicates that a particular teaching approach advances the learning of students by one standard deviation above the mean. This is typically associated with advancing achievement by one year or improving the rate of learning by 50 percent; it can also refer to the correlation between a variable and achievement of approximately 0.50. Hattie (2018) submits that "the effect size of 0.4 sets a level where the effects of innovation enhance achievement in such a way that we can notice real-world differences, and this should be a benchmark of such real-world change" (p. 17). At 1.29, more than triple the benchmark standard set for real-world impact, it is safe to say that the implementation of RTI is a high-leverage move for schools. Behavioral intervention programs, according to Hattie (2018), yield a 0.62 effect size.

While Hattie's methods and conclusions have come under some scrutiny within academia (Simpson, 2017; Slavin, 2018; Wiliam, 2016), the conclusions for practitioners are no less compelling. Researchers can debate the minutiae of effect sizes and rankings, but those in the field need only know whether an innovation or practice has a high degree of effectiveness. Nothing is implemented in a vacuum, so practitioners must pay close attention to contextual nuances, established norms, and implementation choices. Even if a margin of error were to be considered for both RTI and behavioral intervention programs, the effect sizes would likely still be well above the 0.4 threshold of effectiveness.

On the behavioral side of the ledger (where we find student attributes like responsibility), positive behavioral interventions and supports is one of the most widely adopted frameworks (Horner & Sugai, 2015). Utilizing an identical three-tier framework to that of RTI and MTSS, PBIS has been shown to be associated with improved student behavioral and academic outcomes (Bradshaw, Waasdorp, & Leaf, 2012; Bruhn, Gorsh, Hannan, & Hirsch, 2014; Freeman et al., 2016). Implementing PBIS with fidelity has also been associated with improved school climates (Bradshaw, Pas, Debnam, & Johnson, 2015) that are proactive, are data driven, and utilize an instructional approach to developing social competence. The shift from a consequence-driven, reactionary mindset to an instructional one emphasized with PBIS would have schools mirroring the academic teaching, learning, feedback, and intervention processes for social-skill development.

Research is one thing; implementation is another. While the research foundation for each of the three-tier frameworks (RTI, MTSS, and PBIS) is abundant, it is still up to schools to implement with finesse in order to balance the fidelity of ideas with the contextually relevant nuances that personalize the systems and processes. Poor implementation planning can give the impression that an idea is bad when, in fact, the idea has been warped by a shortsighted or too-loose approach that deviates from even the most basic non-negotiables. Emphasizing one aspect (such as the orthodoxy of the research) over the other (such as contextual relevance) is less favorable than finding the balance between the two that ensures both fidelity and finesse to maximize student outcomes.

A Three-Tier Framework

There are two fundamentals that emerge from a three-tier framework. The first is that one size doesn't fit all. As cliché as that expression may sound, the three tiers bring that perspective into full view. The second fundamental, which is a by-product of the first, is that the intensity of any intervention must match the intensity of the present challenge. These two fundamentals imply that when holding students accountable, schools must consider the intensity of the challenges, including the challenges the students face in their lives outside of school. Not every student who misses a deadline, for example, misses the deadline for the exact same reason. The circumstances that surround (and potentially inhibit) the students' abilities to follow through with their responsibility will vary. As a result, our responses must also vary accordingly. Figure 3.1 (page 48) shows an example depiction of the three tiers. Assuming effectiveness within the previous tier, the number of students reduces within each subsequent tier.

Tier 1: Core Program

Tier 1 is about prevention. While interventions are often seen as post-instructional responses, the most efficient and effective intervention is prevention. Employing high-quality, research-validated practices helps teachers ensure that any challenges students face are not the result of misguided instructional choices. For interventions to be effective, they need to be the right fit for the behavioral challenges students have, and that means knowing the why behind the behavioral challenges. By ensuring universal access to a core program that involves teaching appropriate behavior and providing preventions to support students in advance (Buffum, Mattos, & Malone, 2018), teachers will maximize opportunities for student success before challenging behaviors have a chance to emerge.

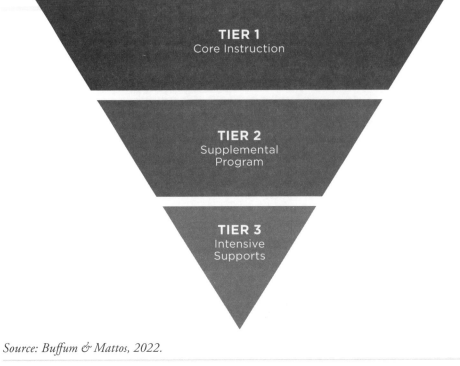

Source: Buffum & Mattos, 2022.

Figure 3.1: The three-tier RTI at Work model.

Tier 2: Supplemental Program

No matter how effective Tier 1 systems and practices are, some students will require a more intensive response. Tier 2 provides these students with a more targeted level of support to match their needs. These secondary supports are often delivered in a group-based format where students who present similar challenges receive the same support. Generally, Tier 2 interventions, whether academic or behavioral, are short-term interventions that are driven by the goal of a seamless return to Tier 1, where students can then continue with the effective core program. Students should not be labeled as Tier 1, 2, or 3. They are either responsive or unresponsive to each tier's strategies and interventions and therefore emerge needing Tier 1, 2, or 3 supports. Tier 2 is an existing program of support that students can rapidly access should it be necessary; it is not a generic purchased program or online resource. Tier 2 is a system that the school develops organically for the purpose of targeted group-based interventions.

Tier 3: Intensive Supports

Tier 3 is the tier of personalization. While Tier 2 fits students into an existing program of support, Tier 3 builds the program of support to the student's specific needs since the student was not successful with either Tier 1 instruction and Tier 2 interventions. Tier 3 is most specific and granular, focusing on skill remediation. Tier 3 interventions occur over the longest time period in terms of both singular sessions during any given school day and the duration of the implementation. Each subsequent tier is more labor intensive than the last, so it is important that schools not predetermine the need for Tier 3 interventions without first implementing and completing Tier 2 interventions.

Anticipation and Proactivity

The implementation of any three-tier framework is inherently anticipatory. The framework assumes that regardless of what strategies, practices, and processes a school implements in Tier 1, they won't be equally effective for every student. This, ironically, should be somewhat comforting to teachers, as an unrealistic expectation of universal effectiveness can leave teachers feeling inferior when some students do not respond positively to some interventions. Being able to predict a degree of ineffectiveness actually prevents teachers from overreacting (feeling inferior) when their students struggle to learn.

Because teachers can anticipate some students will struggle, they proactively plan their responses for each level, with increased instructional intensity in Tier 2 and increased personalization in Tier 3. While teachers may not be able to account for all students' unique circumstances or idiosyncrasies, schools can put predictable systems and routines in place so teachers can be ready when students need more support. This creates a more settled environment for students as well. Students know that they will receive supplemental support for any academic or behavioral misstep. Without this anticipatory, proactive approach, interventions get left to chance, are inconsistently implemented, or are inadvertently omitted altogether.

The Academic-Behavioral Link

The relationship between low academic performance and high rates of antisocial behavior is not straightforward. However, according to researchers Kristen P. Kremer, Andrea Flower, Jin Huang, and Michael G. Vaughn (2016), there is enough of a correlation between the two to substantiate the overarching claim that achievement and behavior are inversely related and that this relationship can have lasting effects. Kremer and colleagues (2016) assert this relationship is strong enough to make the case that educators "should consider providing intervention in both domains to the same students; a reasonable way to do this may be to couple response to intervention and positive behavioral interventions and supports in schools" (p. 102). In other words, behavioral interventions should be part of any academic support planning, and academic interventions should be part of any behavioral support planning; whether either realm plays a small, medium, or large role within the plan will be dependent on each student's unique circumstances.

Educators would be wise to use a Venn diagram of academics and behavior to visualize this planning; this diagram would help them figuratively establish that the influence one has over the other is minimized but that attention toward one is accounted for in the other realm. In other words, while we seek to separately assess and report on academic achievement and behavioral competence, we simultaneously must recognize the influence each has on the other.

RTI at Work and Redefining Student Accountability

RTI is the three-tier framework that provides a picture of how a school will redefine student accountability. It provides a view of the day-to-day work that happens through prevention, more support, and personalized support within the three tiers.

Tier 1: Prevention at the Core

Tier 1 instruction and support are designed for all students. At this tier of prevention, schools establish a baseline from which the interventions increase. While it is alluring to focus on the relatively small percentage of students who present the most challenging antisocial behaviors, schools must not skip this foundational tier.

At Tier 1, schools establish the social norm of responsibility as a universal expectation by clearly defining it, creating observable success criteria, proactively teaching it, and following up on chronic missteps that interfere with student growth. Schools should establish the systems, practices, and data routines that allow for a comprehensive approach. *Systems* set predictable routines for teachers, which translate into predictable experiences for students. The systems for teaching, providing access to support, and following through (for example, the responsibility instruction schedule, data collection, and intervention access) sustain the new routines long term; they are not about diminishing professional autonomy. The predictability established by our schoolwide systems makes it less likely that teachers will waver over time. It's easy to be energized and focused at the beginning of the school year; it's quite another thing to maintain that energy as the school year progresses.

While systems exist behind the scenes and are the exclusive domain of educators, *practices* are how we interface with students. These practices are what emerge from the systems. Any actions that directly involve students (for example, responsibility lesson plans, intervention strategies, and restorative strategies) are practices. Systems create the routines; practices bring them to life. Here, schools will decide how they will teach responsibility, what will happen (often progressively) should students fall short repeatedly, what interventions they will utilize, and how they will redirect students to more prosocial actions.

Data, while often thought of as being synonymous with spreadsheets, refers to information that is often gathered through observation. Data ensure that educators make decisions not haphazardly but deliberately through the use of relevant information. This way, decision making is justifiable and not vulnerable to educators' idiosyncratic feelings about what should be done. Schools need data routines for gathering information, for interpreting the information, and for assessing the long-term success and sustainability of their efforts.

Data, systems, and practices are not separate silos; each one is dependent on the other two for effective implementation.

Tier 2: More Support

Tier 2 provides schools with an answer to the question of how to respond when some students inevitably emerge as irresponsible. At Tier 2, educators increase the time, intensity, and frequency of interventions, interactions, instruction, and monitoring. While Tier 2 is more labor-intensive than Tier 1, schools can make it efficient through use of a group-based implementation model rather than one-to-one interventions. With a program approach, students with similar support needs are grouped for follow-up instruction. Remember, Tier 2 intervention systems are often collectively pre-established by the staff (intervention specialists, administration, and learning support staff), which makes student access almost immediate, should it be necessary.

Tier 2 is where more intensive social-skill training occurs—more of what was implemented in Tier 1. This includes more instruction and practice, more frequent monitoring and interaction, more frequent reinforcement of prosocial demonstrations, more precorrection, and more intensive focus on academic supports linked to the irresponsible behavior.

A small team of teachers, administrators, counselors, intervention specialists, and other professionals with at least some behavioral support expertise (such as social workers) implements and monitors Tier 2 interventions. It is most advantageous that this team be a subgroup of educators and professionals connected to a school's leadership team (or guiding coalition in a PLC), as that makes seamless communication of Tier 2 interventions' effectiveness more likely. This small team will also take the lead on data collection, data interpretation, and the subsequent adjustments the gathered information warrants.

Tier 3: Personalized Support

Despite the effectiveness of Tiers 1 and 2, some students will remain unresponsive to the instruction and intervention and will therefore require a more personalized approach. Whereas Tier 2 gives students immediate access to an existing system, structure, or routine within the school, Tier 3 tailors the support system, structure, or routine to the needs of the individual student. Tier 3 is not special education; it is a highly personalized approach that considers what students' unique antecedents (triggers) are and why students are maintaining the irresponsible behavior (what is reinforcing the behavior) to create an individualized support plan.

Teams effectively accomplish this individualized support using a functional behavioral assessment (Hirsch et al., 2020; Sugai, Lewis-Palmer, Hagan-Burke, 2000) where they map out a behavioral sequence to reveal the root cause of the irresponsible behavior. Figure 3.2 outlines what a behavioral sequence would typically look like (Loman, Strickland-Cohen, Borgmeier, & Horner, n.d.).

SETTING EVENT	ANTECEDENT (TRIGGER)	ANTISOCIAL BEHAVIOR	MAINTAINING RESULT
What other situations, circumstances, or conditions make the situation worse?	What are the circumstances that directly lead to the antisocial behavior?	What behavior is causing concern?	What makes the antisocial behavior the most efficient and effective response for the student?

Source: Loman et al., n.d.

Figure 3.2: Functional behavioral assessment sequence.

Functional behavioral assessments are labor-intensive to create and implement, so again, it is wise to invest in Tier 1 and 2 interventions. Educators need to be sure that the effort associated with a functional behavioral assessment is truly necessary.

The first step in the functional behavioral assessment sequence is to identify the antisocial behavior or behaviors. Then, through a series of interviews (with teachers and the student) as well as a period of observation, the team develops an initial hypothesis about what triggers the behavior (antecedent) and what reinforces it (maintaining result). Note that Figure 3.2 shows how antisocial behaviors emerge in real time; however, the inquiry and subsequent determination of the sequence happens in order of importance: What's the behavior, what triggered it, and what maintains it? Finally, the team determines the setting events. These events don't cause the antisocial behavior, but they make the situation or circumstances worse. Note that determining the setting events may not even be possible since setting events may occur beyond the purview of the school. For example, a student's irresponsible behavior may increase in frequency, intensity, or longevity immediately following a stay with one parent in a shared-custody situation. The team may be able to determine such a setting event only if the student volunteers that information during functional behavioral assessment conversations. Becoming familiar with the student's life outside the school context deepens team members' relationships with the student and strengthens the team's ability to develop a relevant plan.

Once the team has determined the sequence, the team aims to help the student learn the skills of responsibility through the behavioral support plan. The plan will initially focus on identifying prosocial *acceptable alternatives* that initiate the process of the student eventually developing the *desirable response* (such as meeting deadlines). Acceptable alternatives find the balance between the antisocial behavior and the desirable behavior. On the one hand, the acceptable alternative does fall short of the desirable action; on the other hand, it represents a step toward eventually reaching the desirable outcome. For example, rather than arriving to school having not completed an assignment or having missed a deadline, the student (or family, depending on the student's age) could email, text, or message the teacher the night before explaining the situation. Asking for more time to complete an assignment, messaging that the assignment was too difficult or complex, or even messaging that the assignment is not done because the student had to work late is at least one step closer to the established schoolwide expectation of meeting deadlines.

PBIS-SEL Integration

Some schools think that they have to choose between implementing the three tiers of PBIS and implementing social-emotional learning. Rather than viewing this as a binary choice, considering PBIS and SEL as a continuum is more thoughtful. PBIS is more teacher-centric and may be a more advantageous place to begin when schools are experiencing low overall rates of prosocial behavior and social norms are relatively loose. However, schools experiencing high overall rates of prosocial behavior and tightly followed social norms may choose to begin with the SEL competencies and the development of self-regulatory skills. Again, when schools view PBIS and SEL as a continuum, they can synthesize the strengths of both approaches into a comprehensive approach that has independent, prosocial, and self-regulatory learning as the desirable outcome.

The biggest obstacles to this integration are the proponents of each approach who often fail to acknowledge the strengths of the other approach (Bear, Whitcomb, Elias, & Blank, 2015). Proponents of SEL often fail to acknowledge the strength in the strategic use of reinforcement in PBIS; proponents of PBIS often disproportionately focus on immediate or short-term successes without thinking of long-lasting impact (Bear et al., 2015). Rather than staking out an unmalleable position, schools would be wise take advantage of the strengths of both.

Taking Action

The essential advantage of the three-tier RTI framework is that it provides an organizing structure for schools to act. Teaching responsibility is identical to teaching academic skills. Once teams establish the expectation and subsequent criteria, teachers can proactively teach those criteria through all their contextual iterations and determine the appropriate reactions to any antisocial demonstrations. This way, teachers ensure that they hold students accountable for the missteps but also redirect and support the students through a restorative practice.

Establish Expectations and Criteria

The first step is to establish the expectation of responsibility in Tier 1. It is unreasonable to hold students accountable to invisible expectations, so schools must articulate expectations and the associated criteria. The criteria allow for a level of specificity and the contextualization of responsibility. Students need to be taught that being responsible or being held accountable means, for example, that they are organized, on time, prepared, consistent, and disciplined; they own their mistakes; and they stay current with the established pace of learning.

Once a school has established expectations and criteria, teachers teach this information. Teaching criteria for social skills often involves a contextualization where lessons focus on how to be organized, on time, prepared, consistent, and disciplined; how to keep pace; and how to take ownership of mistakes. Where the expectation is unreasonable for some students (such as some students with identified special needs), the appropriate and applicable accommodations (possibly modifications) are put in place; otherwise, the expectation and criteria are taught to all students as part of the Tier 1 approach to establish the foundational social norms.

After that, a school establishes systems or routines that provide regular reinforcement and feedback to the students for prosocial demonstrations. Like with academic skills, it's important that teachers utilize effective feedback that acknowledges strengths (the student's specific demonstrations of responsibility) and identifies aspects that need strengthening (places where the student fell short). Reinforcement is a social exercise where adults provide regular, predictable feedback for prosocial behavior with the goal of increasing the likelihood that the criteria of responsibility become embedded and the norm. We'll take a deeper dive into reinforcement in chapter 4 (page 65).

Determine Interventions and Supports

Once a school has established the Tier 1 system of teaching and reinforcing responsibility, the school must then plan its Tier 2 and 3 responses. Remember, no matter how effective your Tier 1 systems are, a small percentage of students will be unresponsive to the schoolwide or classwide efforts in the first two tiers.

While teachers can informally manage infrequent demonstrations of irresponsibility, chronic issues require a more intensive response in Tier 2. Because students often emerge from Tier 1 with similar needs for skill development, the first line of action is small-group intervention. This approach allows for efficiency in scheduling time for learners, and it gives students an opportunity to learn from one another. The key to Tier 2 support is the increased predictability and frequency of instruction.

Educators need to provide regular and predictable feedback for students' prosocial demonstrations in Tier 1. To students, however, the feedback can potentially feel a bit random since a teacher who is regular and predictable with feedback will likely not interact directly with the same students every single day. A hallmark of a student success at Tier 1 would be longer stretches of time with little to no direct, positive adult feedback—that they demonstrate prosocial behaviors whether they are being monitored or not. At Tier 2, students who need more frequent interaction and reinforcement receive it in regular intervals. Again, the intensity of the interventions must match the intensity of the presented need, so it is likely some students will need feedback for prosocial behavioral demonstrations at more predictable intervals (daily or even hourly).

Despite all efforts, some students will emerge as unresponsive to Tier 2 interventions, which means their interventions must be personalized. At Tier 3, intervention specialists, behavioral support teachers, and counselors (or the identified responsible personnel) will personalize the interventions to individual students in hopes that each student grows toward demonstrating more responsible behavior. The work at Tier 3 involves understanding the root causes of misbehavior, the circumstances that create unique challenges, the conflicting reinforcements that are interfering with positive growth, and the incremental steps needed toward success. Tier 3 often requires expertise beyond that of a typical classroom teacher. The labor-intensive nature of Tier 3 should remind schools that efficiency and effectiveness at Tiers 1 and 2 are essential if there is to be sufficient time to support students who emerge as unresponsive and needing personalized support in Tier 3. Artificially escalating the number of students needing Tier 3 interventions by not reaching the necessary success thresholds (such as 80 percent at Tier 1 and an additional 15 percent at Tier 2) through ineffective implementation will leave teachers and administrators in a perpetual reactionary state.

Determine the Frequency of Interaction and Observation

As a general rule, when the intensity of the interventions increases as we move through the three tiers, so does the frequency with which we monitor student responsibility. Monitoring is essential if teachers and administrators are going to provide students with feedback for their authentic demonstrations of the identified prosocial behavior. Teachers can't provide guidance, feedback, affirmation, or redirection if they aren't observing their students.

Establishing routine around data cycles is also important as schools gauge the effectiveness of their efforts to increase student responsibility. At some point, we have to determine whether our efforts have paid dividends. Has our approach to teaching student responsibility actually developed more responsible learners? It's important not to conflate the idea of data with a binder full of spreadsheets; data are simply the observable, relevant, and accurate pieces of information that allow teachers and principals to confirm the degree to which interventions are being effective. For example, when teachers and administrators observe an increase in responsibility (such as being prepared for learning) or respectful interactions among students, they will have greater confidence that their efforts are producing the desired results.

Schools would be wise to think about monitoring data monthly, weekly, and daily for each tier within the framework. Of course, this schedule of data progression is a suggested guideline, not an absolute one; schools need to find data-monitoring rhythms that make sense for the students within their context, both collectively and individually.

In Tier 1, adults should be regular and predictable in their interactions with students for responsible behavior. In addition, monthly cycles of data monitoring provide the information needed for broad and deep analysis. Because Tier 1 focuses on the entire student population, it could take a month or so to produce a clear picture of where the students are collectively in terms of their responsible behavior. For Tier 2, weekly cycles of data analysis might be more appropriate since the interventions (teaching, coaching, and redirection) are more frequent. As the size of the group shrinks with each tier, it becomes possible for schools to increase their monitoring of prosocial behaviors; a weekly cycle for Tier 1 would likely not produce an adequate sample of the entire student population.

For Tier 3, consider daily monitoring to ensure educators notice, acknowledge, and reinforce students' most incremental steps. Because students in Tier 3 have been unresponsive to both schoolwide efforts (Tier 1) and targeted group-based efforts (Tier 2), their irresponsibility communicates to teachers that the intensity of the intervention does not match the intensity of their individual challenge. A personalized plan for improvement often requires real-time adjustments that can occur at a moment's notice (depending on the intensity or severity of the behavioral misstep), so having a daily data-monitoring cycle is most helpful.

The Big Picture

A three-tier framework encompasses all behavioral attributes: student responsibility, respect, self-directedness, work ethic, and the ability to collaborate (to name a few). In the three-tier framework, these attributes can be taught, nurtured, developed, refined, and reinforced through systems and fundamental practices, as well as monitored through data collection processes. The collective effort around the identified behavioral attributes sends a clear message: the whole child matters, not just the academic portion.

Establish Schoolwide Social Norms

Establishing schoolwide social norms (for example, positive personal and interpersonal behavioral expectations) is the critical first step of Tier 1. The schoolwide effort begins by prioritizing a few (typically three to five) behavioral characteristics that are applicable in all settings. These settings can include ones in the community, as a desirable outcome of this effort would be that the characteristics become not just *what students do* at school but *who they are*. The prioritization of three to five attributes does not mean other attributes don't matter; they do. The prioritized attributes simply act as statements about where there is the most leverage for students (in other words, what attributes are most universally applicable) and where the school will spend the majority of instructional time dedicated to developing behavioral attributes. For example, when a school highlights responsibility, respect, self-directedness, and productive work ethic as the attributes on which to focus, the school is saying, "These are the attributes we are going to purposefully teach, develop, nurture, monitor, and report on."

As schools implement a purposeful instructional model for behavior, they must predict students' degree of unresponsiveness to the Tier 1 efforts so they can plan for the follow-up interventions. We know Tiers 2 and 3 will be necessary, so we can plan for how we will make our instruction and intervention more granular. For example, as part of developing responsible students, a school might focus on teaching students why organization is part of being responsible, what organization looks like, and what some universal strategies are that support student growth (for example, how to plan to meet deadlines when a project is due). At Tier 2, given that the universal lessons of Tier 1 proved ineffective, students will work in a small group where the instruction is tailored to the specific habits of disorganization that the students exhibit (for example, more specific and hands-on planning for those students who procrastinate or for those who rush to finish). The more intimate setting allows for instruction to be targeted to a group of students who have similar traits of disorganization.

Once the instructional plan is designed, schools need to create opportunities for students to practice the attributes, demonstrate them, and grow their skill with these attributes. Many of these opportunities will emerge naturally through day-to-day routines (for example, observing which students do and do not arrive to class prepared with all of their materials), which means teachers need simply plan for, be aware of, and notice these demonstrations. Where opportunities may not naturally occur day to day, teachers create opportunities (for example, mapping out a plan to complete a science project on time). If we have declared a behavioral attribute to be important, then we must back up that declaration with action.

Ensure Norms Are Culturally Expansive

To be most inclusive, schools must actively solicit varied cultural perspectives when defining their social norms. Traditionally, North American schools define appropriate behavior through a White, Eurocentric lens. Teachers have thought students who act outside those norms to be misbehaving despite behaving in alignment with the cultural norms learned at home, with extended family, or within the community. Social norms need to be expanded to reflect varied cultural perspectives. Through the most expansive approach, school norms will reflect the diversity that's found within the student population.

Teacher educator Zaretta Hammond (2015) writes that *culturally responsive teaching* is about ensuring culturally and linguistically diverse students who are often marginalized in schools build their skills to reach rigorous outcomes. Traditional schoolwide social norms have left those who are culturally diverse feeling *othered* (excluded). Culturally expansive social norms serve to ensure that all learners, regardless of their cultural background, begin from a place of acceptance and inclusivity.

Focus on Student Investment in Social-Emotional Competencies

Students' age will determine the degree to which the students can invest in themselves and become more self-regulatory, but despite that, student investment in learning prosocial behavior has to be the goal from the outset. Schools with high rates of antisocial student behavior will likely take an instructional, hands-on approach (such as direct instruction, monitoring, and feedback) to establish prosocial norms. However, once those prosocial norms are cemented, schools have to keep going by transitioning to a model that is student centered, directed, monitored, and reported. Rather than being told by the adults that "these attributes are important," students recognize the importance of developing aspects of themselves beyond academic performance. This is rarely easy to accomplish, but it remains the ultimate goal.

Schools can accelerate this transition by shifting focus from *expectations* to *SEL competencies*. As students begin reflecting on their self-management, self-awareness, relationship skills, social awareness, and responsible decision making, teachers can facilitate a transition from "here's what we expect" to "here's what we want you to reflect on." While the development of prosocial attributes may start from the outside in, schools should land at a place where students grow, sustain, and refine these attributes from the inside out; this means teachers create or support the protocols for student introspection. Schoolwide expectations would remain the non-negotiable foundation and provide the substance for reflecting on the SEL competencies. For example, if self-directedness is an established, expected attribute, teachers might ask students to reflect on their level of self-directedness through a self-awareness protocol.

Remember, the goal is that students exhibit the attributes beyond the school setting and without supervision. Students should feel they are being empowered, not controlled. Yes, some control might be needed at the beginning of program implementation to reset the social norms of the environment, but the absence of antisocial behaviors doesn't mean a prosocial environment has been established; the absence of *negative* doesn't equal *positive*. Intentional prosocial action by students is obvious evidence that students have developed the necessary habits and skills for now and later.

Summary

The three-tier framework of RTI, PBIS, and MTSS is the perfect organizational structure for a truly schoolwide approach to redefining student accountability because one size never fits all. Some students act in accordance with prosocial norms, while others need some interventions and supports to learn more appropriate social skills; still others need more intensive, personalized support that matches the intensity of their unique circumstances.

The key is to leave nothing to chance. If schools want certain behavior, we have to teach that behavior through a proactive instructional model. We identify the desirable student attributes, along with their observable criteria, to ensure that, just like with academic learning, the expectations are transparent and obvious. Despite the anticipation that the schoolwide instructional model will be ineffective for a small group of students (those who emerge needing Tier 2 and 3 supports), the instruction is for the entire student population. We first need to establish the floor from which the intensity of interventions increases, knowing that the interventions' intensity must match the intensity of the presented challenges. Rather than predetermining which students need which tier of interventions, we hope for the highest positive response rate at Tier 1 since each subsequent tier is more labor-intensive.

The characteristics that embody the schoolwide social norms need to be as culturally expansive as possible. We have to interrogate the Eurocentricity on which most schoolwide expectations in North America have traditionally been established. By involving students from the outset, we can ensure that the established social norms (and especially the adjacent criteria) truly reflect the cultural diversity found within the school. This student investment in establishing the culturally expansive attributes lays the groundwork for the eventual transition to a self-regulatory process anchored in the SEL competencies. The transition from teacher-centered to student-centered practices and processes is the most desirable outcome that results in students' embodying (not just *doing*) the attributes when outside the school setting and when under no supervision; those attributes become who the students are.

Questions for Learning Teams

1. What quotation or passage encapsulates your main takeaway from this chapter? What immediate action (small, medium, or large) will you take as a result of this takeaway? Explain both to your team.

2. Reflect on your school's current routines. Are there existing systems, structures, practices, or norms that could make the redefining of student accountability easier to begin?

3. Given your school's current routines, what are the most pressing needs (personnel, collective expertise, revised priorities) that your school must reconcile to maximize success at redefining student accountability?

4. Does your school need to establish schoolwide prosocial norms through a quite instructive model (such as PBIS), or can your school begin with prioritizing a student-centered approach to the SEL competencies? What evidence do you have to support your assertion?

5. Is your (and your colleagues') current relationship with data (comfort level in gathering, examining, and effectively using data for decision making) great enough that you can seamlessly transition to redefining accountability? If not, what needs to be done to reconcile that?

6. Evaluate your school's current social norms. Are they very culturally expansive, somewhat culturally expansive, minimally culturally expansive, or not culturally expansive? What should your school's next steps be in either establishing or refining culturally expansive norms?

Part II:

How to Get There

CHAPTER 4

Teaching and Reinforcing Responsibility

Identifying and teaching clear expectations for behavior reduces ambiguity for both students and staff as well as working toward the shared goal of a positive school culture.

—KENT MCINTOSH, ERIK J. GIRVAN, ROBERT H. HORNER, KEITH SMOLKOWSKI, AND GEORGE SUGAI

We educators know from research and practical experience that there is a link between academic success and behavior. We understand that academic success is often partially the result of behavioral or social success, and behavioral or social success is often partially the result of academic success. This understanding sets the foundation for a synthesized approach to redefining student accountability. Schools that have the goal of learning for all must take a proactive approach to redefining student accountability because behavior is so linked to academic performance. This chapter focuses on that foundation of behavioral learning, although redefining student accountability should not be a siloed approach. Effective and efficient instruction, assessment, and feedback will be crucial in serving each and every learner.

Teaching Responsibility Schoolwide in Tier 1

Maximizing success in redefining student accountability begins with a schoolwide approach using a three-tiered RTI system. Tier 1 provides a proactive foundation of prevention on which the more intensive interventions of Tiers 2 and 3 are based. The process of redefining responsibility in Tier 1 includes (1) establishing the expectation, (2) teaching responsibility proactively, (3) monitoring student behavior, and (4) providing ongoing positive reinforcement.

Establishing the Expectation

Establishing the expectation for accountability means both identifying and defining responsibility as a schoolwide behavioral expectation—a social norm of the school. Students hear the word *responsibility* all the time, but as a concept, it might not be clearly defined for them. We can't leave responsibility as a "we'll know it when we see it" idea in schools. A school might define responsibility as follows. (This is an example, not the only possible definition.) The definition is written in first person so students understand the concept in relation to themselves.

> To be responsible means that I create my successes and I cause my missteps. Rather than blaming others or offering excuses, I am answerable for my actions and choices.

Once the definition is established (or even co-constructed), the school needs to clarify it so students understand that the definition applies only if they are *responsible* for what happened. There are, of course, situations where others cause students to arrive late, miss assignments, be unprepared, and so on. If students truly are not responsible for the behavior, then they are not accountable and, therefore, not answerable for it.

The next step to laying the foundation is to define the expectation in all directions, meaning articulating what responsibility looks like (1) to oneself, (2) to others, (3) to learning, and (4) to the school environment. Table 4.1 illustrates how the working definition is put into perspective within every dimension of school; the age and maturity of the students will determine how simple or sophisticated the language within should be.

Defining responsibility in this way personalizes the concept so it is not too abstract, and it allows students to understand how they can demonstrate responsibility. After presenting the four-way definition established by the school (potentially co-constructed with some students), individual teachers would be wise to lead a

Table 4.1: Responsibility in Four Directions

Self	I create my own successes, and I cause my own missteps. Rather than blaming others or offering excuses, I am answerable for my actions and my choices.
Others	My actions positively contribute to the potential academic and social success of others. I am mindful of how my actions and choices could potentially impact others, and I use that awareness to guide my decisions.
Learning	My actions positively contribute to the learning environment for both me and others when I actively participate in all learning opportunities and remain supportive of my classmates' academic needs. I ask for help when I need it, and I offer help when others need it.
School Environment	My actions positively contribute to a clean and safe physical environment within the school.

discussion of other ways that students can demonstrate responsibility. For example, a teacher could ask the students, "What other ways can we show responsibility to ourselves, to others, to learning, or to the school environments that are not listed?" These behavioral examples will reveal authentic understandings of responsible behavior and need not be standardized among all teachers, just aligned with the expectations. Schools, especially those implementing PBIS, will often use a behavioral matrix for this purpose. The behavioral matrix is advantageous, as it articulates the expectations, contextualizes them, and provides specific behavioral examples. While a typical behavioral matrix would contextualize all the behavioral expectations, the example in table 4.2 (page 68) isolates responsibility as one behavioral expectation.

It's not possible to list each and every setting throughout the school. The most prominent, high-profile areas should be specified, but the "all settings" category should be included so students understand that no school settings are exempt. Also, it is important to emphasize to both students and staff that the matrix is not an answer key. The behavioral examples within the matrix are just that—examples. They are not the *only* ways to exhibit responsible behavior. Having conversations about other ways that responsibility can manifest in various settings is crucial.

Table 4.2: Behavioral Matrix for Contextualizing Responsibility

SETTING	BEHAVIORAL EXAMPLES
All Settings	• Admit, correct, and learn from your mistakes. • Seek and encourage peaceful and mutually agreeable solutions to conflict.
Hallways	• Be mindful of the people and space around you as you move through the school. • Keep to the right as you move quickly, yet safely, to your next location.
Outside	• Use outside equipment only for what it is intended. • Be safe and make choices that positively contribute to everyone's experience.
Cafeteria	• Clean up after yourself by putting trash and recycling in the appropriate containers. • Actively prevent or report any damage, vandalism, or graffiti.
Library	• Leave things as you found them or as they are supposed to be. • Contribute positively and productively within the library.
Assembly	• Be attentive to the established expectations for the assembly (for example, listening to an informational speaker or participating in a pep rally). • Actively listen and productively contribute to the overall experience.
Bus	• Sit appropriately and follow all safety guidelines. • Use an appropriate voice when communicating with others.

Establishing the expectation of responsibility must include a purposeful and authentic effort to be culturally responsive and expansive. This has to occur at the start of defining responsibility and the contexts. Cultural differences emerge when considering what responsibility looks like, sounds like, and feels like in various cultures, especially those present within the school community. One caution here is to avoid casting specific cultures as monoliths; there is no singular way to define, for example, Indigenous culture. The best sources for this cultural responsiveness when it comes to responsibility (or any other expected social norm) are the students. Schools need to engage students in conversations about the cultural nuances within their families and their cultural norms. Keeping certain principles at the forefront of these conversations reveals the cultural nuances that impact behavioral expectations. Table 4.3 provides nine cultural values (Menzies, 2018) and example questions that can assist in identifying cultural nuances.

Table 4.3: Nine Cultural Differences and Example Questions

CULTURAL DIFFERENCE	EXAMPLE QUESTIONS TO ASK STUDENTS
1. Individualism Versus Collectivism	Do most people within your culture define themselves in terms of the individual or in terms of the collective? Does your culture value individual uniqueness or contribution to the group?
2. Power Distance	In your culture, do people who have less power than others expect and accept inequalities (high power distance—only a select few can and do have power), or do people of your culture believe that inequalities should be minimized (low power distance—power is shared)? Is the power base within your culture typically stable and scarce (high power distance—only available to a select few), or is the power base shared and transient (low power distance—available to all)?
3. Uncertainty Avoidance	How comfortable are most people within your culture with ambiguity? To what degree do most people within your culture need predictability? Are there strict behavioral norms and an intolerance for unorthodox ideas or behaviors?
4. Time Orientation	Are most people within your culture focused more on long-term outcomes or on short-term outcomes? Is there a tendency to favor short-term pursuits while neglecting longer-term implications?
5. Gender Egalitarianism	Would you consider your culture to have high gender egalitarianism (people of different genders share social and emotional roles) or low gender egalitarianism (people of different genders have distinct social and emotional roles)?

continued →

6. Assertiveness	Does your culture generally value assertive, dominant, and "tough" behavior, or is that behavior seen as socially unacceptable? In your culture, does who you are or what you can do matter more? Are saving face and being subtle valued in your culture?
7. Being Versus Doing	Does your culture tend to value fitting into the world as it is (being) or changing, directing, or exploiting the world (doing)? Are most people in your culture motivated by quality of life (being) or financial success (doing)?
8. Humane Orientation	Does your culture tend to value others more than the self (high humane orientation) or the self more than others (low humane orientation)? Is self-enhancement (low) or the enhancement of others (high) the predominant thought within your culture?
9. Indulgence Versus Restraint	Is it generally acceptable in your culture to pursue activities purely for the sake of enjoyment (indulgence), or is it more important to adhere to strict social norms (restraint)?

Source: Menzies, 2018.

There are several considerations to keep in mind when using the questions in table 4.3 to establish culturally responsive behavioral expectations and norms.

- Casting any cultural group as a monolith is problematic. The questions are designed to examine tendencies, though there are always exceptions to every general rule.

- The choices that appear in the table are not necessarily binary, though they are presented that way. Within almost every culture, we are likely to find a sliding scale from one side to the other.

- We will need to adjust the questions based on the age and language appropriateness of the students. Younger learners may work more effectively with examples than direct questions. It's also wise to proactively involve parents with learners of any age, but especially with younger students.

- We should think of this conversation as being holistic rather than as involving nine separate areas. The goal is not to accentuate the differences or to inadvertently create a culture war within the classroom where students compare (and critique) one another's cultures. A more holistic approach—a discussion of how people can be more culturally inclusive—keeps the focus on the positive outcome.

- The questions are merely a starting point for a more nuanced, context-dependent conversation about cultural responsiveness; they are not predictors of individual behaviors or values.

Culturally expansive conversations about schoolwide expectations can be tricky to navigate simply because we don't want to inadvertently get it wrong and remain exclusive. However, the need for culturally expansive conversations about school-wide expectations, including responsibility, is long overdue. Cultural differences and nuances will drive an important and necessary discussion about what is prosocial and acceptable with in the school context. What is expected must be inclusive. Allowing the process to unfold without any time constraints is important to authentically let the community know that we are serious about cultural expansiveness. Rushing the process could result in many seeing the entire process as performative.

Teaching Responsibility Proactively

In schools, teachers make academic learning goals clear. They identify the pathway that progresses students from simple learning to sophisticated learning, they identify criteria for success, they create opportunities for students to receive feedback on their progress, and they measure the degree to which students have met the identified learning goals. That entire process is applicable to behavioral attributes as well.

The use of examples and non-examples is the key to bringing expectations—academic or behavioral—to life. Criteria, whether in an academic rubric or a behavioral matrix, are abstract on their own. In classrooms, academic exemplars bring criteria to life and allow students to clearly visualize what the descriptive statements within a rubric mean; the examples found within a behavioral matrix do the same. Examples and non-examples can be effective in creating contextual norms without creating uniformity. Most students can memorize the meaning of the word *responsibility*; that's the easy part. The more important part is knowing what that means and, therefore, what that looks like. The following is an example of a quick conversation that could unfold between a teacher and a student whom the teacher randomly engages in a hallway.

> Mr. Donovan: "Good morning, Jasmine."
>
> Jasmine: "Good morning."
>
> Mr. Donovan: "Random question—what is one of our school's most important characteristics that we've been focusing on this year?"

> Jasmine: "Responsibility."
>
> Mr. Donovan: "What would responsibility to yourself look like here in the hallway?"
>
> Jasmine: "Walking to class or wherever I'm going as quickly as possible and without hanging out in the hallway. Then I won't be late and other students can move through the hall and they won't be late either."

In the example, Jasmine illustrates her understanding of the expectation of responsibility within a specific context. Teachers need not get hung up on whether the student's response matches what's in the matrix or rubric. What matters is that the example they provide makes sense and is aligned with the expectation.

Not every discussion has to be monumental. A teacher could engineer a conversation about granular aspects of responsibility, such as by asking, "What if your plan to finish an upcoming project is undermined by an unexpected visit from your grandparents?" or "How do you approach a group member who is not following through on their responsibilities?" Once the expectation and criteria have been established, potential scenarios for real-time instruction are endless. Teachers just need to be aware of opportunities and take advantage of them when the opportunities present themselves.

Another approach to teaching responsibility is to teach through subject-based content (for example, through characters in a novel) or through personal dilemmas students might face. Teachers can engage students in contextual and relevant conversations that grow the students' collective repertoire in how an expectation might play out. In English language arts, for example, a teacher could ask students to argue for or against the assertion that Darrel "Darry" Curtis is the most responsible character in S. E. Hinton's novel *The Outsiders*. In social studies, when examining Indigenous landrights, a teacher could ask, "What does it mean for a society to take responsibility for past actions when the current members of the society are not personally responsible for the previous wrongdoings?" Any attribute can be examined on a macro level within the context of specific subject areas.

If a more formal process is desired, teachers (or whole faculties) could develop lesson plans to implement on a predictable cycle (for example, once per week or once per month). Table 4.4 (adapted from Lewis, 2014) shows a structure for developing lessons to more formally execute instruction on behavioral attributes. Teachers can use a more sophisticated template for academic planning if desired. It's up to the individual teacher or the school to decide the specific format.

Table 4.4: Responsibility Lesson Plan Components and Details

LESSON COMPONENT	DETAILS
Tell	Identify the specific aspect of responsibility (such as meeting deadlines) and the specific criteria.
Show	Demonstrate or model the characteristic (teacher or student). For example, a student who is highly proficient in the skill could explain their process for examining their calendar when planning to complete a major project. During a demonstration, the teacher could demonstrate non-examples.
Practice	Students practice the skill. For example, the teacher leads a broader conversation about time management and proactively examines the academic focus of the upcoming few weeks to ensure students remain current with all assignments.
Review	The class collectively summarizes the big ideas of the lesson. For example, the teacher asks students to determine the top five ways to stay organized in advance of deadlines.
Follow Up	Use naturally occurring future opportunities to reinforce the skill. For example, when a major project is assigned or students are facing an exam week, the teacher engages students in reminders and refinements of how to be organized and responsible in advance of the future opportunity.

Source: Lewis, 2014.

Teaching desired behavioral attributes should be purposeful, but it need not be complicated or extensive. The identified attribute and students' maturity level may determine the lesson's sophistication. While high school students might focus on the global application of responsibility (for example, social responsibility to the world), K–3 learners might focus on responsibility to themselves. This is not to suggest that young learners can't be globally focused; they can. Rather, it suggests that the examples may focus on what's relevant given students' age and maturity.

Monitoring Student Behavior

After teaching comes ongoing reinforcement and monitoring of students' prosocial displays of the prioritized characteristics. The day-to-day school experience is filled with opportunities for teachers to monitor and reinforce responsibility in action. Teachers might be surprised to realize the instructional priority of teaching responsibility creates a level of awareness that allows them to notice displays of responsibility they might have overlooked before. Implementing weekly lessons can have the added benefit of creating a focus for observation, collective support, and prioritized interactions; for example, there could be a theme of the week that highlights specific aspects of the prioritized attribute. Teachers shouldn't ignore other characteristics of responsible behavior. The specific lesson of focus simply takes priority that week. Teachers can always take advantage of natural opportunities that come up, but an ongoing, purposeful approach ensures the focus on specific characteristics is sustained.

Starting the school year with a "blitz on behaviors" that puts an intense focus on behaviors is unhelpful and unsustainable throughout the entire year. This blitz creates the illusion that these behaviors and attributes only matter during the first months of school. Everyone collectively exhales in relief after that "behavior stuff" is over. Schools might place a little extra focus on behaviors at the beginning of the year, especially with the youngest learners within the school (such as sixth graders in middle school) since the expectations need to be contextualized for them. But a continual and purposeful effort is what maximizes the long-term impact.

Ongoing monitoring can also include data collection. This doesn't mean keeping detailed spreadsheets and over-quantifying attributes; rather, as with any instructional effort, verifying behavioral instruction's effectiveness matters. At the most basic level, if schools claim they are teaching more than just academic standards, such as responsibility, teachers have to be able to support that claim with evidence. Their emphasis when teaching responsibility should be on relevant and specific information as opposed to numerical data. Teachers often collect data to answer a specific question. For example, data-focused questions pertaining to responsibility could include, "Has the number of late or missing assignments decreased?" or "Am I seeing students' use of proactive communication increase when they anticipate not being able to meet expectations?" We must gain useful information without creating an onerous data collection system or becoming distracted by the system. We need good information to assist us with decision making about our effectiveness.

Providing Ongoing Positive Reinforcement

Unfortunately, the idea of positive reinforcement has been conceptualized in many different philosophical and idiosyncratic ways. In education, a dichotomy has emerged. Some view reinforcement as a *thing* (a tangible that is distributed), while others view it as an *effect* (a naturally occurring result of a particular set of circumstances). People agree that the key to increasing academic achievement is feedback (Ruiz-Primo & Li, 2013), whether that is from the teacher (external) or from the students themselves (internal), but mentions of external feedback for behavioral attributes often get branded as coercion or manipulation; we can't have it both ways. When working with students on behavioral attributes, we must stick to the science and not become distracted by societal definitions and connotations.

One misunderstanding of positive reinforcement is that it is always good; in fact, it is not. Reinforcement is neutral and strengthening. It increases the probability that similar behaviors occur again (Sugai & Simonsen, 2020). This can include increasing the probability that antisocial behaviors occur again. Society leans heavily toward the idea that reinforcement is "good" and consequences are "bad," but goodness and badness can be judged only in relation to the desirable outcome. If the goal is to increase the likelihood that a student is more responsible going forward, then reinforcement would be good, but it's not inherently good. It's deemed to be good because it would support the goal. If, for example, a student acts inappropriately in class and receives an avalanche of positive peer attention, then it's probable the peer attention will reinforce the antisocial behavior and therefore increase the chances that the student acts inappropriately the next day. In this case, the reinforcement is definitely not good.

Figure 4.1 (page 76) provides a brief overview of the principles of behavior that underpin an effective approach to behavioral improvement (Sugai & Simonsen, 2020). It is critical to consider figure 4.1 through a scientific lens and resist the temptation to allow societal connotations (for example, reinforcement is always good and punishment is always bad) to influence your understanding. Also, note that the references to *something* in the left column in figure 4.1 refer to something social (such as time or attention) and not something tangible (like a reward).

To determine the success of any behavioral intervention is to identify whether the goal was to increase or decrease the likelihood of a certain behavioral attribute and then determine whether the intervention produced the desired result. Reinforcement and punishment, as defined in figure 4.1, are neither good nor bad; they're neutral and deemed good or bad when assessed against the desired outcome. That's why the same intervention can serve as a reinforcement for one student and a punishment for another. Temporarily removing Liza from science class decreased her disruptive behavior (Liza enjoys science) while temporarily removing Connor increased his (Connor does not like science). This example illustrates that "time out," if you will, is only effective when there is a desirable "time in" context.

	REINFORCEMENT	PUNISHMENT
	Anything that increases the likelihood that a behavior will occur again	Anything that decreases the likelihood that a behavior will occur again
POSITIVE *To give something*	**Positive Reinforcement** Increased likelihood of a behavior occurring again after something is given (For example, Maria's teacher gave her positive feedback for her responsible behavior. Maria's responsibility increases.)	**Positive Punishment** Decreased likelihood of a behavior occurring again after something is given (For example, Hakeem's teacher had Hakeem come back to class at lunch to finish the previous night's homework assignment. Hakeem's lack of homework completion decreases.)
NEGATIVE *To remove something*	**Negative Reinforcement** Increased likelihood of a behavior occurring again after something is removed (For example, Alex's teacher removed him from mathematics class for disruptive behavior. Alex dislikes mathematics. Alex's disruptive behavior increases.)	**Negative Punishment** Decreased likelihood of a behavior occurring again after something is removed (For example, Lucy's teacher moved her to another group in class because she was off task and spent too much time talking with friends. Lucy's off-task behavior decreases).

Source: Sugai & Simonsen, 2020.

Figure 4.1: The principles of behavior.

A second misunderstanding of positive reinforcement is that some see *reinforcement* and *reward* as synonymous. Positive reinforcement is a social interaction, whereas a reward is often (not always) a tangible thing. Conversations about rewards can be polarizing and bring visceral responses, and there is much debate about the use of tangibles or tokens to influence behavioral choices. Some assert that the use of external tangibles diminishes intrinsic motivation (Pink, 2009), but assessing intrinsic motivation is challenging since assessors have to either make inferences based on what's observed or assume that what a person is reporting is accurate; we'll save this debate for another day. For the purpose of redefining accountability, any use of tangibles should be squarely focused on usage by adults as simply a tool to remind them to be regular and consistent with their feedback for demonstrations of prosocial behavior.

According to the science of behavior analysis, reinforcement and punishment are *effects*, not *things* that are applied. Education professors George Sugai and Brandi Simonsen (2020) warn that using generic definitions and synonyms leads to misunderstandings and misapplications:

> The concept of reinforcement in education is often seen as synonymous with terms like "recognition," "reward," and "acknowledgement." The use of general definitions and synonyms that are not conceptually grounded decreases precision, weakens implementation, and shapes false perceptions about the utility and appropriateness of reinforcement, especially for students with challenging problem behavior who require highly individualized and precise behavioral supports. As a result, educators may develop misrules and misapplications of reinforcement, such as (a) "students shouldn't be coerced into doing the right thing for rewards"; (b) "external praise and recognition damage the development of intrinsic motivation and develop an overreliance on extrinsic incentives"; and (c) "reinforcement is a form of bribery and has no place in the classroom." (p. 79)

Meaningful improvement in student behavior will happen when educators can shed the misunderstandings and generic synonyms and replace them with nonjudgmental conceptualizations of the effects of reinforcement and punishment. The misunderstandings only lead to implementation errors.

Tangibles

Educators need to be regular and predictable with their feedback for prosocial behaviors. However, it is easy to get caught up in day-to-day busyness and forget. Tangibles can act as physical reminders to educators. The most cynical (and inappropriate) use of a tangible is to distribute it for prosocial behavior with zero interaction—to just give a student a thing when they are acting appropriately. That's an implementation error, and that misuse should not be blamed on the existence of tangibles. If a tangible is not accompanied by an authentic interaction with descriptive feedback about what prosocial behavior the teacher observed, then the use of the tangible is inappropriate and should be criticized. When we can reframe the use of a tangible as a reminder to the adults (rather than a token for students), the tangible can exist against the backdrop of meaningful social interaction that increases the likelihood a student will develop prosocial attributes.

Descriptive Feedback

We know that descriptive feedback is key to improving academic learning, so why would behavioral improvement be any different? Teacher-student interactions, however, can sometimes lack the descriptive part of behavior-based feedback. In the name of efficiency, teachers sometimes resort to a quick barrage of "good jobs" with no description of what they specifically observed or what was good about it. And, most importantly, the feedback lacks the positive adult attention (such as eye contact, time, and authentic interactions) that makes the exchange meaningful to the student. The research on effective feedback unequivocally shows that descriptive feedback lays the groundwork for improved student proficiency (Black & Wiliam, 1998; Hattie & Timperley, 2007; Kluger & DeNisi, 1996; Ruiz-Primo & Li, 2013; Shute, 2008; Stobart, 2018). Remember, the foundation for improving student responsibility (and other behavioral attributes) is that these skills can be taught and nurtured like academic skills.

Consistency matters when it comes to reinforcement. While the approach at Tier 1 may, at times, feel somewhat arbitrary and haphazard for students, it is regular and predictable for the adults. Adults won't regularly or predictably interact with the *same* students at Tier 1, but they will regularly and predictably teach responsibility in a proactive way, monitor student behavior, and provide ongoing positive reinforcement. Perseverance at Tier 1 will bring about permanent changes. Students (as well as adults) do not simply snap out of old habits. Popular folklore suggests it takes twenty-one days to form a new habit; neuroscientist and psychologist Brian King (2020) asserts there are too many unknown variables to definitively say how long it takes to establish a new habit. However, common sense suggests it's really hard to change our behavior. Breaking these habits takes time, so an unwavering approach is needed for long-term success.

Targeting Behavioral Intervention in Tier 2

Despite educators' best, most consistent efforts, some students will remain unresponsive to Tier 1 strategies. Tier 2 provides *more*—more frequent instruction, monitoring, feedback, reinforcement, reteaching, and redirection—to a relatively small, targeted group of students. The effective and efficient student response rate for Tier 1 is typically set at 80 percent or higher, meaning 80 percent of students will not need

Tier 2 intervention. When more than 20 percent of students require Tier 2 intervention, this indicates there is a Tier 1 issue. According to Alyssa M. Van Camp, Joseph H. Wehby, Bailey A. Copeland, and Allison L. Bruhn (2021), it is important to ensure "there are adequate classwide levels of Tier 1 supports be in place before implementing Tier 2 intervention" (p. 62). For example, a school with one thousand students could reasonably expect that two hundred students will need more intensive group-based instruction. Most schools would have the appropriate staffing to support that percentage of students. But if the positive response rate at Tier 1 were only 70 percent, then that same personnel, space, expertise, time, and money would need to support three hundred students, which might not be possible. Conversely, if the Tier 1 response rate were 90 percent, then the same personnel, space, expertise, time, and money would be available to support one hundred students at Tiers 2 and 3. Imagine how much deeper and more sustained the support could go for fewer students. This is why an investment in Tier 1 strategies and interventions is necessary, despite the fact that we can predict Tier 1 interventions will be ineffective for some students.

Targeted Group-Based Instruction

The main characteristics of Tier 2 interventions are that they are *targeted* (focused on the specific needs of individual students) and *group-based* (implemented using small-group instruction). However, it is a common misperception that Tier 2 must be group-based; it doesn't necessarily have to be. Being group based is about efficiency in delivery. Tier 1 is whole group (class or schoolwide) and Tier 3 is individual, which leaves a small-group model as the in between—a group of students who have similar intervention needs. Putting students in groups when they have dissimilar intervention needs because of a belief that Tier 2 needs to be group based is not appropriate and does not reflect the spirit of balancing the efficiency and effectiveness of delivery at Tier 2.

According to the Center on Positive Behavioral Interventions and Supports (2023), Tier 2 is characterized by the following.

- **Increased instruction and practice with self-regulation and social skills:** Regardless of the intervention, Tier 2 supports include additional instruction for key social, emotional, and / or behavioral skills. An important outcome of Tier 2 interventions is when students can regulate on their own, when, where and under what conditions particular skills are needed and can successfully engage in those skills. Once data indicate a positive response to the intervention, students learn how to monitor and manage their own behavior.

- **Increased adult supervision:** Tier 2 supports include intensified, active supervision in a positive and proactive manner. For example, adults may be asked to move, scan, and interact more frequently with some students, according to their needs. This can be accomplished with simple rearrangements across school environments.

- **Increased opportunity for positive reinforcement:** Tier 2 supports target expected behavior by providing positive reinforcement more often. For example, students who participate in a Tier 2 Check-in Check-out intervention engage in feedback sessions with their classroom teacher and other adults in the school as many as 5–7 times per day. Many students view this positive adult attention as reinforcing and as a result may be more likely to continue engaging in expected behaviors.

- **Increased pre-corrections:** At this level, another key practice to prevent problem behaviors is to anticipate when a student is likely to act out and do something to get ahead of it. For example, specifically reminding students of classroom expectations. These pre-corrections might be gestures or verbal statements delivered to an entire class, a small group of students, or with an individual student. Pre-corrections set students up for success by reminding them, prior to any problem, what to do.

- **Increased focus on possible function of problem behavior:** It is important to consider why students engage in certain behaviors in order to align Tier 2 interventions best suited to their needs. When they know what motivates students to behave a certain way, teachers can help them find alternatives to their unwanted behavior.

- **Increased access to academic supports:** Some students receiving Tier 2 behavior support may need additional academic support, too. Often challenging behavior serves the purpose of allowing students to avoid or even escape academic tasks that are beyond their skill level. Academic intervention along with behavioral supports may be needed to improve student success.

It should be noted that the word *increased* precedes each of the characteristics of Tier 2 behavioral support. Before contemplating an overhaul to their approach, schools would be wise to consider that many students emerge as unresponsive to Tier 1 not because Tier 1 strategies were ineffective; rather, they emerged unresponsive because the frequency and intensity of Tier 1 did not meet the presenting needs of the students. It is always possible that a different approach might be necessary, but it's more efficient to begin Tier 2 with a more frequent and more intense approach.

Intervention in the Classroom

Tier 2 is a supplement to Tier 1, not a replacement. As such, Tier 2 can occur on a much smaller scale. It is true that Tier 2 often happens through a formal intervention schedule and is implemented by a small team with more behavioral expertise to ensure students receive the more granular instruction they need. Tier 2 can also occur within the classroom. Any time a teacher increases the instruction and self-regulatory opportunities, the supervision, the opportunities for positive reinforcement, the precorrections, the academic supports, and their consideration of function (for example, what is being gained or avoided) for a small percentage of students in their classroom, they are engaged in Tier 2. There can be a tendency to think Tier 2 need be an epic endeavor, and while sometimes it is, teachers can often support and redirect students to more prosocial behaviors in real time within their classrooms.

Personalizing Intervention in Tier 3

Tier 3 is for personalization after the schoolwide (Tier 1) and targeted (Tier 2) approaches prove ineffective. Remember, the intensity of intervention must match the challenge a student is presenting. When students are unresponsive to intervention, it is wise for educators to consider whether the lack of improvement is more about a mismatch of intervention than a willful act of defiance, though willful acts of student defiance do exist. However, even what appears to be a willful act of defiance on the surface is still most likely an indication of an unmet need.

As discussed in chapter 3 (page 45), personalization begins with understanding a student's behavioral responses, what events or situations maintain those responses, and how to teach the student a more prosocial way to fulfill the unmet needs. For example, if the challenging behavior is irresponsibility, teachers will want to identify the *antecedent* (what triggers the irresponsibility) and the *maintaining result* (what reinforces the antisocial behavior). Figure 4.2 shows an oversimplified behavioral sequence to illustrate this point.

SETTING EVENT	ANTECEDENT (TRIGGER)	ANTISOCIAL BEHAVIOR	MAINTAINING RESULT
Projects that are group based rather than individual	Project-based learning opportunities	Failure to meet deadlines for projects	Avoiding difficult and complex assignments

Figure 4.2: Behavioral sequence example.

Setting events make the existing behavioral responses worse. In this example, the *project*, not the fact that it is group based, triggers the undesirable response. The key for planning is to help the student learn more prosocial actions, such as asking for support when a project seems challenging. By asking for support, the student is technically able to initially avoid doing the challenging task on their own since someone (the teacher or another student) assists them. The long-term plan, of course, would be for the student to work independently and lean into challenging tasks, but getting there will often take some time. That is the complexity of Tier 3.

At Tier 3, the instruction, monitoring, feedback, reinforcement, reteaching, and redirection happen multiple times throughout each day, sometimes hourly (or less). Both intensity and personalization are maximized in Tier 3. Consequently, implementation is often inefficient since no two students at Tier 3 are likely to have the exact same needs. So again, this is why jumping to Tier 3 supports is unwise in most cases. By proactively investing in efficient and effective practices at Tiers 1 and 2, schools can have greater confidence that the students they are personalizing for at Tier 3 are the ones who truly need it.

Summary

Leave nothing to chance; purposefully establishing the expectation of responsibility is the first step toward developing students who are responsible for their actions. When schools accompany the expectation with a complete articulation of what that expectation looks like (criteria) within various contexts and under specific circumstances, they position themselves to fulfill the promise of teaching more than just the academic curriculum. Establishing culturally expansive expectations through an inclusive process will ensure there is no othering within the school where students feel their cultural norms are at odds with the schoolwide expectations.

However, the expectation of accountability alone is not enough; schools need to proactively teach the expectation through both formal and informal processes. Opportunities to informally teach responsible behaviors and attributes occur on a daily basis. Teachers will find ample opportunities to infuse responsibility discussions into normal routines and daily school experiences, such as before introducing a major project or while hypothesizing unexpected setbacks that put the ability to meet deadlines in jeopardy. Simultaneously, schools might also consider a formal lesson structure (such as once per week) to proactively teach students the habits and attributes that make one responsible. This can be especially impactful at the transitional grades where students are entering a new level (such as in grade 6 for middle school) and a new building.

The reinforcement of student responsibility is how these new habits will become permanent. Reminding ourselves that reinforcement is an effect (not a thing) ensures that our examination of any teaching or intervention is focused on whether it increases the likelihood that the student will continue acting responsibly going forward. Educators must be regular and predictable with their feedback (positive reinforcement) for any behavioral attribute they wish to help develop in students. The quality of the interactions is also critical. Interactions must include time, attention, and a purposeful description of what the educator observed. This signals to students that behavioral attributes matter.

Educators would be wise to anticipate that, despite all that purposeful effort, a small number of students will emerge as being unresponsive to the initial Tier 1 efforts. For those unresponsive to the Tier 1 approach, a more targeted, group-based approach (Tier 2) that emphasizes more frequent instruction, monitoring, feedback, reinforcement, reteaching, and redirection will be necessary. Still, some students will need an even more personalized approach that is tailored to their individual needs (Tier 3). The intensity of the intervention must match the intensity of the student's presented need; if it does not, the intervention will not be successful.

Questions for Learning Teams

1. What quotation or passage encapsulates your main takeaway from this chapter? What immediate action (small, medium, or large) will you take as a result of this takeaway? Explain both to your team.

2. To what degree has responsibility been established as an expectation within your school context? Is it simply a stated expectation with no substantive efforts underpinning it, is it an expectation with intentionality and purpose behind it, or is it somewhere in between?

3. What would be the most favorable model for implementing a formal instructional process around responsibility (and other behavioral attributes) in your context?

4. How culturally expansive and inclusive are your school's student behavioral expectations? Do you see an opportunity to reset or expand those expectations through a more inclusive process? Could you see your school using some, most, or all of the nine questions of cultural differences to guide the process?

5. What mindset do people within your school context have regarding reinforcement? Do you think most see reinforcement as a thing or an effect? What hurdles do you anticipate in trying to shift the collective mindset so people see positive reinforcement as a necessary part of redefining student accountability?

6. How equipped do you think your school context is to support those students needing Tier 2 and Tier 3 supports? Do you have the needed think time, space, budget, personnel, and expertise?

CHAPTER 5

Correcting Irresponsibility and Supporting Responsibility

Discipline, unlike punishment, is proactive and begins before there are problems.
—LORI DESAUTELS

No matter how valiant our efforts, there are going to be students who act irresponsibly. Knowing this, we can plan for our response, including who might initiate the first intervention. The nuances of each situation (and student) mean predetermining generic responses is futile. However, we can develop a general plan that guides our responses to ensure we don't over- or underreact. This is critical for creating an approach to student discipline that emphasizes support and inclusion rather than removal and isolation.

It is also essential to keep irresponsibility in perspective; irresponsibility is undoubtedly important, but it is not the most egregious act a student can demonstrate. Sometimes, the intensity of our responses to irresponsibility is disproportionate to the nature of the irresponsibility itself. To keep student responsibility in perspective, schools would be wise to develop a schoolwide approach to student discipline that creates a continuum. Following this continuum can create consistency and ensure that responses (and consequences) are not contingent on which adult the student is interacting with. So, while previous chapters began with close examinations of responsibility and then broadened their scope to include other important student attributes, this chapter will do the reverse so that responsibility finds its place among the array of student behaviors and attributes educators encounter.

Discipline, Not Punishment

Within the traditional school context, the words *discipline* and *punishment* are often used interchangeably. When redefining student accountability or reshaping the collective culture around any student behavioral attribute, schools question whether discipline is what adults do to students or how adults guide students. Are students to *be disciplined*, or will they be guided to *become disciplined*?

A Necessary Shift

The word *discipline* is often defined in two ways. One is to *punish or penalize*, and the other is to *train or develop*; these definitions epitomize the shift necessary in schools. While certain behavioral missteps may have natural or logical consequences, we should primarily see behavioral errors as communications of an unmet need. According to the Center for Emotional Education (2017), there is no such thing as misbehavior, and the appropriate way to examine student behavior is to understand this:

> Children (especially young ones) who are experiencing powerful emotions *aren't choosing* actions—they're compelled by their feelings to act in ways that they can't regulate. They aren't *misbehaving*. They're doing exactly as their biology intends. And whether we like it or not, it couldn't be more appropriate for where they are developmentally and what they are experiencing physio-emotionally. (Center for Emotional Education, 2017)

Discipline is about teaching, training, and developing. If we can see antisocial behaviors as teachable moments, then we can create a culture of discipline that emphasizes support and inclusion rather than removal and isolation. Real discipline is what educators do *with* students, not *to* them.

Of course, adults need to exercise some control over the classroom or the school—there needs to be some established order. But when threats of removal and isolation are the primary method to coerce behavioral compliance, educators are more likely to build resentment and damage relationships with students than to actually change their behavior (Morrison, 2015). Compounding this is the fact that there are significant racial and ethnic disparities within school disciplinary practices (Peguero, Varela, Marchbanks, Blake, & Eason, 2018), particularly in the United States, where Black and Hispanic students are suspended at roughly five times the rate of their White peers

(Camera, 2020). While controlling students through fear of punishment can be alluring (and occasionally successful), the adversarial relationship that can emerge between educators and students with a punishment model will do more to alienate students from the learning environment. Fear interrupts normal brain function that allows people to regulate emotions and read nonverbal cues, so even if a student is compliant through fear, the impact on the student's thinking and decision making will make optimal academic performance unlikely.

Many schools *talk about* teaching responsibility, but punishments and consequences too often drive their collective actions. When they instead mainly focus on creating opportunities for students to become disciplined through instructional corrections, social-skill training, and continual reinforcement, the *gotcha* atmosphere that kept students in line evolves into an atmosphere that helps them grow and develop.

The Failure of Exclusionary Discipline

Finding the right approach to school discipline has always been a hot topic in education. But educational policy researchers Bryan R. Warnick and Campbell F. Scribner (2020) argue:

> As schools have grown increasingly bureaucratic over the past century, formalizing disciplinary systems and shifting from physical punishments, such as whipping, to forms of spatial or structural punishment, such as suspension, school discipline has not only come to resemble the operation of prisons or policing but has grown increasingly integrated with those institutions, subjecting children to new levels of surveillance, restraint, and criminalization. (p. 99)

They contend that schools hold a unique place in society and that this heightened emphasis on surveillance misaligns with the ethos of education (Warnick & Scribner, 2020). Once schools are reconceptualized as moral communities (rather than rigid enforcers or managerial bureaucracies), the nature of school discipline can be more closely examined and subsequently aligned with the desirable outcomes. According to Warnick and Scribner (2020), schools are conceptualized as social institutions where "the development of vocational soft skills, the promotion of autonomy, and the acquisition of civic dispositions of community engagement and understanding" are meant to take place (p. 105), and the widespread use of exclusionary discipline tactics is antithetical to those outcomes.

Having studied research comparing traditional and innovative approaches to school discipline, behavior experts Jessica Hannigan and John Hannigan (2016) unequivocally find that the traditional approaches to school discipline are associated with lower achievement, they do not reduce incidents of antisocial behavior, and they fail to make schools safer. Hannigan and Hannigan (2016) state that "in analyzing over twenty years of research on discipline approaches, researchers found that out-of-school suspension and zero-tolerance approaches do not reduce or prevent misbehavior" (p. 40). In fact, suspension and expulsion have been shown to decrease the likelihood a student will graduate from high school on time (Balfanz, Herzog, & Mac Iver, 2007). Researchers Brea Perry and Edward Morris (2014) find that even nonsuspended students' academic achievement is negatively impacted by a punitive context; this collateral damage, they write, is the reason why schools need to eliminate excessively punitive policies and reimagine school discipline through the lens of social integration. The research is overwhelmingly clear: traditional school discipline doesn't work.

With an overwhelming body of research indicating that traditional discipline doesn't work, it is a wonder why so many educators (and adults for that matter) continue to find traditional disciplinary approaches alluring. Special education professor John W. Maag (2001) perhaps hit on the essence of the issue in a way that still rings true. Speculating as to why the punishment paradigm still permeates education and society as a whole, Maag (2001) writes:

> A punishment paradigm has evolved, and been advocated for, since biblical times and is reflected in the proverb "spare the rod and spoil the child." Besides having history on its side, a punishment mentality has been perpetuated for the simple reason that punishing students has traditionally been highly reinforcing to teachers. Punishment often can produce a rapid—although often temporary—suppression in most students' inappropriate behaviors. Furthermore, because punishment techniques may be quickly and easily administered, teachers have found them quite desirable to suppress a variety of classroom disruptions. (p. 176)

Is it that simple—that we more readily accept punitive measures in society, especially when it comes to controlling children? Maag (2001) hypothesizes that another reason punishment is a favored approach to school discipline is that it works for 95 percent of the students. He submits that "most students attending public schools . . . behave fairly well. Consequently, mild forms of punishments, such as the use of verbal reprimands, fines, or occasional removals from the classroom, typically control most students' behaviors" (Maag, 2001, p. 177). So, the false logic that emerges is if mild forms of punishment work for most, then more severe punishments must be the answer for students with the most challenging behavior (Maag, 2001). That false logic is as prominent today as it was at the time of Maag's writing.

The Fallacy of Traditional Consequences

The great fallacy of the traditional model of school discipline is that it is instructional; it is not. The only thing traditional school discipline teaches students is that under the circumstances, they should have behaved differently, but rarely are they taught *how*. A student who is physically aggressive toward another student is unlikely to learn how to control their anger or outbursts simply by being sent home for a few days. Some students, of course, would find this consequence to be a sufficient deterrent, likely because they already have the self-regulatory skills to make that internal shift or some other influence (such as a parent) is teaching them the coping strategies to navigate any similar encounters going forward. The fear of suspension typically motivates only the students who are not getting suspended. Most students are aware of the potential to be suspended under certain circumstances, yet some students still (sometimes repeatedly) act in ways that violate well-established social norms. Clearly, suspension is not always the deterrent or lesson we think it is.

People—not just students—make mistakes both intellectually and behaviorally, and sometimes there are consequences associated with those mistakes. The question is whether educators see behavioral missteps as teachable moments, much as they see academic missteps. It is not a binary choice. Behavioral missteps can have consequences and follow-up instruction that supports the students' growth toward becoming more disciplined. When the inevitable behavioral missteps are seen as *character shaping* rather than *character defining*, schools will create an environment anchored in growth and development.

Students are not mini-adults; they are at various stages of human development and do not have adult brains. An example of this is that preadolescents, or *tweens*, typically replace baby talk with back talk, which is a normal part of their development (Morin, 2020). Tweens are often trying to fit in and look cool, while dealing with increased academic workloads and, of course, hormonal changes. This can lead to some volatile outbursts and some predictable overreactions to seemingly small (from the adult perspective) incidents. At this age, students are also beginning to establish their independence from their parents while navigating their peer connections, which is a combination that predictably leads to misbehavior that can provide the perfect teachable moment. Teaching students how to make more prosocial decisions going forward is what will set them up for long-term success.

A critically important characteristic of the teenage brain is that it is unbalanced when it comes to assessing potential outcomes of situations that arise. The parts of the brain responsible for sensation seeking (the ventral striatum and the orbitofrontal cortex) start growing after puberty begins, while the part of the brain responsible for impulse control (measured in the lateral prefrontal cortex) may not develop completely until early adulthood (Weisinger & Pawliw-Fry, 2015). That means there is roughly a decade where teenagers are challenged to think ahead or balance the pros and cons the way adults do. This at least partially explains why teenagers engage in risky behavior that most fully developed adults would not (Dobbs, 2011). Most adults have at least one moment from their teenage years that they look back on with amazement and wonder, "How could I have thought that was appropriate?"

Schools have the opportunity to keep behavioral missteps in perspective. Perspective is not permission, nor is it an excuse; it means the long-term impact of these acute moments is kept at the forefront of any decision. The imbalance between thrill seeking and impulse control explains, for example, why some students cannot resist the temptation to cheat. Cheating is not OK, but rather than taking a strictly punitive approach, educators have an opportunity to help students recognize their own internal imbalance and strategize how to prevent that temptation from becoming an issue in the first place. Schools will have to decide what the consequences for cheating should be. Perspective will be achieved when those consequences are balanced with the necessary instruction that leaves the students more skilled and self-aware going forward.

The Impact of Trauma

Emerging awareness of the pervasive impact that trauma has on students is another essential element to establishing an effective schoolwide approach to discipline. So many of what have traditionally been labeled as *bad behaviors* or *choices* are now being recognized as logical, rather predictable reactions when certain emotions are triggered.

An Assumption of Trauma

Trauma is more pervasive than one might first imagine. According to the United States' Centers for Disease Control and Prevention (2022), "About 61% of adults surveyed across 25 states reported they had experienced at least one type of ACE [adverse childhood experience] before age 18, and nearly 1 in 6 reported they had experienced four or more types of ACEs."

ACEs fall into three general categories: (1) abuse, (2) household dysfunction, and (3) neglect. According to the Substance Abuse and Mental Health Services Administration (n.d.), "More than two thirds of children reported at least 1 traumatic event by age 16." The statistics on trauma are both consistent and alarming. If roughly two of every three children will experience trauma before the age of sixteen, the most efficient and effective way for schools to operate would be to assume that all students have experienced some kind of trauma.

There is efficiency in assuming all students have experienced trauma. While it might be possible for small schools to assess students for trauma on an individual basis, large schools would likely find it nearly impossible to actively determine whether each student has experienced some kind of trauma. In addition, trauma-informed practices have no downside for those students who have not experienced trauma. Assuming all students have experienced trauma means a more effective shaping of the schoolwide and classwide approaches to discipline in Tier 1 instruction. To assume students have not experienced trauma is risky since educators can't be entirely sure how trauma has been experienced across the student population. The worst-case scenario is likely to play out: the assumption of no trauma when there has been trauma. This could have devastating and potentially permanent consequences on the relationships between the students and key adults in their lives.

Developing a trauma-informed approach to student discipline does not mean letting students off the hook when it comes to expected social norms; rather, it means embedding the appropriate precorrections and contextual supports throughout the approach to account for as many potential triggers as possible. While it may not be possible for schools to account for every single potential trigger (since trauma is deeply personal), the collective expertise and experience within any given faculty makes it likely that *most* potential triggers could be accounted for. Students who have experienced trauma are still expected to follow the established social norms, but the expectations have to be paired with the appropriate amount of support so that the expectations are fair and reasonable.

Something else educators have to contend with is their own trauma. If almost two-thirds of adults have experienced some kind of trauma in childhood, schools would be wise to consider that some of those adults are the teachers who are developing trauma-informed approaches to school discipline. A teacher's trauma makes responding to students' acute reactions more challenging since the student behavior could serve as a trigger for the teacher. Before they are able to fully support the students, teachers may first need to support themselves. School leaders, with the utmost finesse and professionalism, should thoughtfully and purposefully create a safe environment where open and honest dialogue about teacher trauma can occur. The point isn't to violate anyone's privacy or inadvertently trigger teachers; rather, as schools develop their plans for how to approach discipline, it is important to have some predictability as to how the educators will react in certain situations.

If, for example, a teacher was the victim of childhood violence or abuse, any act of violence by students may trigger the teacher, leaving them unable to intervene in the acute situation. Knowing this would help leaders (and all faculty) understand why and how teachers respond the way they do and recognize the limitations of each faculty member's breadth of response options. Again, this has to be approached with the highest sensitivity, but the more aware at least school leaders are, the more knowledgeable they will be of how to support the teachers should they be triggered by any student incidents.

Within the context of approaching school discipline and redefining student accountability, a trauma-informed approach or underpinning is critical to ensuring all students have the greatest opportunity to thrive. There is no shortage of information and opportunities for educators to become more trauma informed. School leaders should make obtaining this information a priority.

Stress-Response Systems

According to brain and trauma expert Bruce D. Perry (Perry & Winfrey, 2021), all functioning of the brain depends on the state a person is in: calm, alert, alarm, fear, or terror. As one's internal state changes, there is a shift in the parts of the brain that are in control. Figure 5.1 highlights the continuum of internal states and the corresponding changes in both dominant brain area and adaptive response (Perry & Winfrey, 2021).

STATE					
	Calm	**Alert**	**Alarm**	**Fear**	**Terror**
Dominant Brain Area	Cortex	Cortex	Limbic	Diencephalon	Brain stem
Adaptive Response	Reflect	Flock	Freeze	Flight	Fight

Source: Perry & Winfrey, 2021.

Figure 5.1: State-dependent brain functioning.

As Perry and Winfrey (2021) explain, when we are well regulated, we spend most of our days fluctuating between the calm and alert states. When we are calm, we are reflective and have little concern for the world outside ourselves; this is where we daydream and are most imaginative. When alert, we focus on something in our external world and seek understanding or perspective from others (our "flock"); we want to know if our being alerted is warranted. Occasionally, we are challenged or surprised, which moves us to the alarm state and has us thinking more emotionally since the lower systems in the brain are now dominant. Our emotions lead to arguments and even personal attacks (Perry & Winfrey, 2021).

When we face a real threat, we regress to fear, and even lower parts of the brain dominate, leaving our problem-solving skills compromised and our focus more finite and immediate. There is little perspective on long-term consequences of our action. Our adaptive strategy here is flight, as we seek to escape the situation at hand. Terror has us acting at our most primal, and our adaptive strategy is fight, as our survival is our singular priority. So from a school discipline perspective, a school's systems of response must seek to keep students in the calm and alert states to avoid a disproportionate acceleration through alarm, fear, and terror.

According to Perry and Winfrey (2021), when a challenge or stress occurs, it puts us out of balance and activates an internal stress response. People who have a neurotypical stress-response system experience a linear relationship between the degree of stress and the shift of internal state. These people would remain calm or in an alert state with daily challenges. They may become alarmed with moderate stress and don't move into a state of fear or terror unless they are facing distress or a threat.

The greater the stress, the more significant the internal shift. However, for someone who has a sensitized stress-response system due to their history of trauma, even the most basic daily challenges will induce feelings of fear; moderate stress can induce a terror response. Rather than experiencing a gradual internal shift, someone with a sensitized stress-response system has a response that sharply moves upward through alert, alarm, and fear with what others might even see as basic challenges and then flattens at the top once they have reached terror. As a contrast, someone who is resilient would have the opposite reaction; their response would remain calm longer only to sharply curve upward under the most extreme stress.

While this is intentionally a surface-level examination of the complex impact trauma has on students, educators must be mindful that students with a sensitized stress-response system will be physically, mentally, and emotionally exhausted from the relentless intensity. Most people's reactions to stress are proportionate to the circumstances. Those who have experienced trauma are quick to escalate from rational thinking to emotional thinking, which explains why some students respond to corrective or disciplinary action in ways that are out of proportion to the circumstances.

A Trauma-Informed Approach

Being trauma informed means school-based corrective or disciplinary actions are proactively guided by the awareness that regardless of the behavioral misstep or violation, the goal is to keep students in the calm and alert states. No matter how severe the antisocial behavior, there is no justification for accelerating the student through the continuum of states, and no positive outcome will result from it. Educators have the opportunity to make things better or worse through their responses. Among the several strategies to creating a trauma-informed environment, four stand out as critical to establishing a trauma-informed approach to student discipline that will benefit all students, especially those who have experienced trauma.

1. Safety

2. Predictability

3. Control

4. Recovery

Nothing will accelerate a student through the different functioning states quite like feeling unsafe will. For those who have experienced trauma, emotional or physical safety is crucial since the traumatic experience likely led to the opposite. According to Lexie Manion (2020), a trauma survivor, those who have experienced trauma tend to think that danger lurks just around the corner, and they may be fearful of trusting others. Their goal, Manion (2020) asserts, is to "take back the power from the situations that have harmed [them]." Regardless of how the students have acted or what the teacher's potential responses might be, there must be no doubt that the students are emotionally and physically safe. Remember, this has more to do with student perception than adult intention; we educators know we mean no harm, but what matters is the students see things that way.

Being trauma informed also means there is a level of predictability within the environment. Having consistency and predictability through our demeanor, expectations, and actions can help put students at ease (Valenzuela, 2021). Predictability comes with the establishment of structures and protocols that take the guesswork out of the day-to-day experience. Uncertainty can leave those who have experienced trauma with the feeling that danger is just a moment away. Remember, surprise is a trigger that leads to alarm, which is where people (not just students) begin to think more emotionally than rationally.

The lack of control students often feel during traumatic experiences can leave them feeling powerless. This can result in an acceleration to the alarm and fear states, which are respectively characterized by the adaptive options of resistance and defiance (Perry & Winfrey, 2021). The resistant and defiant responses are often branded as bad behavior, but reframing them as students' attempts to regain control can help educators keep things in perspective. Educators can also give students some control by finding authentic ways for them to help determine responses to their own behavioral missteps. Students don't have complete control, but they do have some input as to how things will proceed. It could be as simple as answering a question about next steps (for example, "How might we repair this situation?") that gives the students authentic input. "Either you do as I say or you're expelled" does not provide any choices.

Finally, there must always be a pathway to recovery so that the students' sense of belonging is never in question. When responding to behavioral missteps and antisocial behavior, teachers may easily *otherize* students with phrases such as, "We don't do that here." If people don't do that here, and the student just did it, the student may think, "Does that mean I am not part of the *we*?" Traditional, exclusionary disciplinary practices only serve to isolate students from their peers and their context. While there may be cases where time away from school is warranted (for example, to defuse a situation or to allow for thorough planning for students' return), school and district administrators have for too long relied on removal and isolation as the primary means to address misbehavior. The pathway to recovery has to be clear and unobstructed; some students may have certain responsibilities since they are still answerable for their actions, but there is no doubt they are full members of the school community.

Once educators normalize the dispositions and reactions of trauma-impacted students, they will more easily see the students' misbehaviors as coping strategies that grew organically from a mindset of survival. Seeing all behavior as communication makes it easier (never easy, however) for educators to know how to teach the students to cope and be more self-regulatory under stressful conditions.

A Restorative Approach

Many schools are turning to restorative practices as a framework for building school culture, not just school discipline. Like the section on trauma-informed practices, this section is not meant to provide a deep dive into restorative practices; rather, it will highlight some foundational ideas to a restorative culture.

Restorative Practices

Restorative practices are a collection of nonpunitive strategies and processes focused on maintaining, even enhancing, the multitude of relationships within any given context. Specifically for schools, restorative practices ensure that students never sense the relationships they have with educators are wavering, regardless of the misbehavior. Schools have turned to restorative practices as a means for improving the overall school climate, reducing disciplinary issues, and purposefully addressing equity and other social outcomes.

Rather than viewing antisocial behavior as a violation of rules, restorative practices hold that antisocial behavior causes harm to relationships that need to be restored. Restorative practices expert Lauren Trout (2021) suggests four tenets serve as the foundation to a restorative culture:

- **Centering People and Relationships:** Restorative theory scholars argue that meaningful relationships are the most important element of our social fabric. Putting people and their inherent interconnectedness at the center of our work can inform the way our systems, values, and practices work.

- **Trust:** A key relational element that informs restorative practices is trust. Restorative justice is anchored by an inherent trust in people, communities, and their capacity to resolve their own conflicts.

- **Voice and Agency:** Voice, in relationship to restorative justice, underpins fairness, empowerment, and ultimately healing. . . . Simply put, if people feel that they have voice, they are engaged— and if they don't feel they have voice, they are disengaged. Agency, like voice, is a condition of being able to self-determine. In restorative justice, agency allows people to make decisions that can bring healing or repair harm through accountability.

- **Equity:** Focusing on equity means unlearning bias and working to honor and uplift identities, experiences, and histories that are most impacted by systemic oppression. (pp. 14–15)

Relationships are nurtured and restored (if necessary) when these four tenets serve as the foundation for a school's climate. When these tenets become *who we are*, not just *what we do*, educators have the opportunity to reimagine the disciplinary paradigm within the school.

Emerging Research on Restorative Practices

According to researchers John Gomez, Christina Rucinski, and Ann Higgins-D'Alessandro (2021), traditional, exclusionary school disciplinary actions have adverse effects on all students and are disproportionately administered to both students of color and low-income students. School-based restorative practices have been gaining in popularity as a way of addressing the disparities in school discipline (Gomez et al., 2021). While the theoretical research on restorative practices is rich and robust, K–12 education researcher Sean Darling-Hammond and his colleagues (2020) remind us that "the quantitative research regarding the effectiveness of [restorative practices] in schools is nascent and has only recently grown more sophisticated" (p. 295).

The quantitative research on restorative practices, according to the thorough examination by Darling-Hammond and colleagues (2020), generally indicates that schools could reasonably expect a reduction in punitive discipline and problem behaviors (Gregory, Clawson, Davis, & Gerewitz, 2016; Tyler, 2006), a positive impact on racial disparities (González, 2015; Gregory, Huang, Anyon, Greer, & Downing, 2018), and an overall safer environment (Augustine et al., 2018). Other findings (such as in the areas of attendance and academic impact) are mixed. But the general trend of the preliminary research is promising, so it is incumbent on educators to pay close attention to the details of implementation, as ineffective practices may result from implementation errors rather than ineffective ideas.

Prioritized Relationships

Whether a school implements restorative practices or simply takes a restorative approach, the goal should be strengthening the relationships within the school. The emphasis on relationships is certainly not new; however, it is easy to lose sight of amid the busyness of academic work and our own lives as we express disappointment or frustration with how students are behaving. If we ask ourselves, "How will this student emerge stronger and more connected to me and the school community?" as we decide the appropriate course of action, we are sure to maintain a perspective that prioritizes *learning* from the misstep over *consequences* for it.

While there can be consequences for some antisocial behaviors, K–12 students will benefit more from educators' keeping an instructional focus at the forefront. That is because these students are in their formative years. As discussed previously, the assertion that we're teaching is not necessarily always matched with the applicable action; we say we're teaching, but all we're doing may be consequence based. Making it clear that the process of discipline is anchored in improving social competence communicates to students that relationships are important. Educators can send no stronger message of relationships' importance than that.

A Schoolwide Approach

We are all familiar with the concept that children play their parents off each other when trying to get permission to do something, go somewhere, or access a privilege. If one parent says no, then the children try the other in hopes that either the parents aren't on the same page or one has a weaker moment and, maybe even against their better judgment, grants permission. It's the potential inconsistency that children sometimes try to exploit. Similarly, inconsistent educator responses to antisocial behavior create opportunities for students to leverage one educator against another.

Predictability

The key to an effective school disciplinary system is predictability for both the adults and the students. Uncertainty raises anxiety. For teachers, uncertainty about who should first respond to which antisocial behaviors is an unnecessary stress. Everyone in a school should have clarity on who responds first, who contacts families first, when a referral to administration eventually occurs, and when administration is immediately involved. Without that predictability, teachers, especially those with limited experience, are left to guess the appropriate course of action. For students, stress comes from not knowing how any given adult might react. This stress can lead to an escalated mental state that is more emotional than rational. At best, inconsistency will feel unfair to students; at worst, it will feel like a personal attack.

Inconsistency means students can win or lose the "teacher lottery" in that the intensity of the response they experience depends on which adult catches them behaving antisocially. Not only can educators be inconsistent with one another, but they can also be inconsistent with themselves. Our humanity leaves us susceptible to over- and underreacting, depending on our mood. We tolerate more on some days than on others. These emerging pathways of least and most resistance can result in students' forming a cynical view of educators and lobbying for certain teachers (where possible) to avoid what they perceive to be the strictest environments.

The lack of a predictable system can also leave a school vulnerable to inconsistencies due to leadership changes. With no system in place, a new principal can create a seismic shift in how the school responds to antisocial behavior. A change in leadership will bring about some adjustments (that's to be expected), but with an established system, the principal will have a foundation for assimilating into the school culture and routines. Should any changes or enhancements be desired, the principal is more likely to suggest them based on the current system, not on impulsive reactions to any acute situations.

Office Versus Classroom

A hallmark of an effective and proactive schoolwide approach to discipline is being clear on which behaviors are classroom managed and which behaviors are office managed. This distinction concerns the first point of interaction or intervention. Behaviors identified as *classroom managed* are initially handled by the classroom teacher, or by the attending adult should the behavior occur during unstructured time within the school day. *Office-managed* behaviors result in an immediate referral to administration. This system creates predictability for educators to avoid potential inconsistencies with how individual situations are managed. Predictability for students and families avoids the uncertainty that can come when a school's approach to student discipline is determined from moment to moment.

Figure 5.2 is an example of how a school could create a distribution of office- versus classroom-managed antisocial behaviors. Each school should go through the process of discussing the distribution of responsibilities so that all people involved take full ownership in executing the approach. Readers are not privy to the hours of conversation and debate that resulted in the system shown in figure 5.2. Some readers may disagree with the distribution of behaviors and the responsibilities that go along with it; that's fine. Each school must build the system that works for it.

CITY CENTER HIGH SCHOOL SCHOOLWIDE DISCIPLINE PLAN

MINORS: Minors are handled by the attending staff member. Chronic minors could result in a referral to the school administration.

- Inappropriate assembly behavior
- Inappropriate bus behavior
- Defacing school property
- Disrespect toward other students
- Misuse of electronic devices
- Food theft
- Inappropriate gym behavior
- Inappropriate hallway behavior
- Incomplete homework
- Lateness
- Littering

- Noncompliance
- Misuse of personal equipment
- Lack of preparation for class
- Pushing
- Skateboarding in the bus loop
- Smoking or vaping on school grounds
- Swearing
- Talking out of turn
- Teasing or making derogatory remarks
- Wandering the halls during class time

MIDDLES: Middles are initially handled by the attending staff member. Chronic middles will result in a referral to the school administration.

- Abuse of school equipment
- Cheating
- Inappropriate clothing
- Inappropriate internet sites
- Inappropriate print material
- Inappropriate representation of the school (on field trips, during sports, and so on)

- Invasion of adult space
- Lying
- Misuse of matches or lighters
- Misuse of trust
- Poor parking lot behavior
- Plagiarism
- Use of racial slurs
- Skipping

Figure 5.2: Example schoolwide discipline plan.

continued →

MAJORS: Majors result in an immediate referral to the school administration.

- Inappropriate behavior toward a substitute
- Bullying and intimidation
- Unsafe bus behavior to and from school
- Cheating on an exam or major assignment
- Dangerous use of a vehicle
- Defiance
- Use of illegal substances (such as drugs or alcohol)
- Fighting
- Physical aggression

- Nonemergency use of a fire alarm or calling 911
- Inappropriate off-campus behavior (at lunch)
- Safety concerns (dangerous behavior)
- Sexual behavior
- Sexual harassment
- Swearing at an adult
- Theft
- Vandalism
- Weapons

Figure 5.2 illustrates a progression along three levels of misbehavior: (1) minors, (2) middles, and (3) majors. Some schools might choose to use only two, others maybe four. Again, each school must organically devise a system that works for its context. Adapting another school's plan short-circuits important conversations and pivotal decision-making moments, which is likely to result in less ownership—and perhaps less understanding—of the system. It is important to note that what distinguishes a minor from a middle is that a chronic minor *could* result in a referral to administration, whereas a chronic middle *will* result in such a referral.

Once a school has established its distribution of responsibilities, the school might consider a response guide to ensure the predictability and consistency that are desired. Figure 5.3 outlines what a potential response guide might look like. Guidelines differ from rules or policies in that they *guide* decisions but are always open for interpretation given the unique students, specific incident, and other contextual considerations involved. No discipline policy should ever take the decision making out of the hands of the educators or simply be clinically applied.

The distinction for minors is between infrequent and chronic errors. Rather than using numbers, which are too prescriptive and restrictive, making this consideration allows for situational nuances to play an important role in decisions. There is, for example, an easily identified distinction between arriving late to school five times in one week and arriving late five times in five months; they are not the same and should not be treated as such.

CITY CENTER HIGH SCHOOL SCHOOLWIDE DISCIPLINE PLAN RESPONSE GUIDE

MINORS: Minors are handled by the attending staff member. Chronic minors could result in a referral to the school administration.

Infrequent errors:

- Remind students of the expected behavior and why the expectation exists.
- Be specific; communicate what was observed.
- Help students identify possible replacement behaviors to avoid future errors.

Chronic errors:

Chronic errors are defined as regular, repeated, and frequent behaviors that occur over a short period of time.

- Seek input or guidance from colleagues, case managers, counselors, or administration.
- Contact the parent to discuss the inappropriate behaviors and strategies to resolve them. A parental discussion is required prior to a referral to administration.
- Document incidents, responses, and so on in the student database.

Referrals to administration for level 1 behaviors must be done with an office discipline-referral form.

MIDDLES: Middles are initially handled by the attending staff member. Chronic middles will result in a referral to the school administration.

First occurrence:

- Discussion with the student about the importance of the expected behavior
- Natural consequence or restitution by the student
- Documentation of incidents, responses, and so on in the student database
- Informal notification to administration; parental contact if necessary

---

Figure 5.3: Example schoolwide discipline plan response guide.

continued →

Second occurrence:

- Discussion with the student about the importance of the expected behavior

- Natural consequence or restitution by the student

- Documentation of incidents, responses, and so on in the student database

- Informal notification to administration; parental contact recommended

Third occurrence:

- Referral to administration

Referrals to administration for middle behaviors must be done with an office discipline-referral form.

MAJORS: Majors result in an immediate referral to the school administration.

Any occurrence:

- Referral to administration

Referrals to administration for major behaviors do not require an office discipline-referral form.

Middles are handled a little more procedurally, although the steps do identify several points where informal notification of administration can occur so that referrals don't appear out of nowhere. It's important to note that City Center school faculty decided that three occurrences of the same middle behavior results in a referral; a different school might make a different decision. Again, this is a guideline, not a prescriptive policy. The overriding idea that drives the entire process is open communication among teachers, families, and administration. Once the system is in place, the goal becomes creating a culture where the system becomes unnecessary.

Redefinition of Accountability

Redefining accountability requires more than a monolithic approach of applying consequences. Understanding the variety of student profiles and circumstances allows for real accountability that considers the reasons for missteps. While it's not possible to preplan for every potential scenario, it is possible to examine the issue of accountability more closely. Figure 5.4 outlines a more comprehensive approach to accountability that establishes two things: (1) To the best of the teacher's knowledge, is the student a *can't do* or *didn't do*? and (2) Is the misstep *infrequent* or *chronic*? These four combinations require four different approaches. Can't dos need teaching, while didn't dos need discipline (accountability, not consequences). Likewise, chronic missteps require a more intensive response than those that are infrequent.

	INFREQUENT (TIER 1)	CHRONIC (TIER 2)
	Teacher	**Teacher and Support Team**
CAN'T DO	These are students who occasionally need additional instruction and support.	These are students who need regular, predictable, and more targeted instruction and support.
	Schoolwide System	**Teacher and Administration**
DIDN'T DO	These are students for whom learning must be made mandatory instead of invitational.	These are students who require more targeted behavioral interventions to prevent the problem from persisting.

Source: Schimmer, 2016.

Figure 5.4: Can't-do versus didn't-do and infrequent versus chronic issues.

The following descriptions outline the distinctions among the four combinations (systems) that schools would implement. These descriptions originally appeared in *Grading From the Inside Out* (Schimmer, 2016). Tier 3 is not outlined, as it requires that interventions be personalized to the individual student; *tailor the interventions to the individual student's needs* would be the only description.

Can't Do–Infrequent

Can't do means the student has a skill deficiency preventing them from completing the required assignment. If, on occasion, a student doesn't quite understand the day's lesson and struggles with completing any required tasks, it is the responsibility of the classroom teacher to provide the additional instruction and support. The teacher is in the best position to effectively address the specific learning issue when the student can't do the work. Also, since this profile is inherently unpredictable and rare, the teacher can efficiently act without relying on a system, process, or protocol.

Teachers can respond to those within this profile as needed, and will often need little time to address the issues. Some teachers may ask students to attend an extra tutorial at lunch or after school; others may simply provide a few moments of support and instruction during class time. How involved the intervention is depends on how complex the can't-do issue is. Regardless, the classroom teacher responsible for the original instruction will know best how to address the presented need. That is not to say the teacher shouldn't seek assistance from colleagues to determine the most favorable course of action, but it does mean the responsibility for resolving the issue rests with the classroom teacher.

Can't Do–Chronic

While these students still have a can't-do skill deficiency, the gap in their understanding is predictable and ongoing rather than a one-off (infrequent) situation. Schools need a system or protocol that allows the teacher to work with the student support team to both understand the complexity of the student's learning challenge and know what is most likely to have a long-term positive impact. Despite the repeated nature of the challenge, there is no place for student discipline within this profile. As we have discussed, behavioral consequences for an academic shortcoming are misplaced and misguided.

Students with an individualized education program (IEP) are likely to have the necessary support routines already built into their plans, but non-IEP students for whom gaps in learning are significant and predictable require a shared approach between the teacher and the support team. For example, a teacher might have a scheduled weekly appointment with a student (such as Thursday after school) to ensure that the student is organized, on track, and confident about recently covered and upcoming learning. These students follow the same routine that the can't-do–infrequent students have for individual assignments, but with an additional layer of support. That could mean a scheduled block within which the learning assistance teacher works simultaneously on deepening the student's understanding of the standards at hand and on addressing any learning deficits that may prevent long-term success.

Again, the intensity of any intervention must match the intensity of the challenge. For some students, a preexisting programmed approach may be sufficient. Because the system already exists, teachers can easily adjust the student's schedule to the system and begin the additional support almost immediately. Other students require a personalized teacher response. With a personalized approach, the system must adapt to the student, so much more planning is involved to address student needs readily and reliably. When in doubt, teachers benefit from beginning with a programmed approach to avoid overplanning for can't-do issues that may appear to be more complex than they actually are.

Didn't Do–Infrequent

What distinguishes a didn't do from a can't do is that the student hasn't completed the required assignments despite having the capacity to do so. Teachers sometimes refer to these students as "won't dos" if it seems clear they are defiantly refusing to complete any assignments, though that is challenging to determine definitively. This category is frustrating, and as such, schools would be wise to create a system of shared responsibility that allows teachers to focus more on the can't dos. Didn't-do students understand what to do but haven't done it; teachers should not refer students who require more instruction since the supervising adult may or may not have the expertise to deliver it.

For didn't-do students, we teachers must make learning mandatory, not invitational. Too often, teachers simply invite these students to learn when they continually request the completed work or they make themselves available for additional time and support if needed. Assuming the required assignment is essential, there should be no option to complete it. Teachers need to move from requesting to expecting, and schools need a predetermined protocol for how to respond to students who occasionally don't submit the required assignments. It is important to note that it describes one possibility, not the only choice. Schools must always consider their specific context in terms of resources, space, personnel, funding, student age, and other factors (such as, Do most of the students take the bus home immediately after school?) before determining the best suited approach.

Didn't Do–Chronic

Students who fall into this category are those who are capable of completing the vast majority of expected assignments but continually fall short of that expectation. Rather than more instruction, they require behavioral interventions to support their move toward increased productivity. In one high school I worked in, these students would still go to a work-completion room, but again, they require additional *behavioral* support since their issue is chronic. To be clear, these behavioral interventions do not mean removal and isolation; this support is not about punishing students who haven't completed their work. Behavioral intervention refers more to the broad category of social-skill instruction. The classroom teacher and the administration, and possibly a guidance counselor and other support personnel, share responsibility for these students.

A student may, for example, predictably struggle with deadlines, so they must learn how to pace their work completion or develop a habit of accessing additional support more rapidly in advance of a deadline. The necessary interventions and instruction focus on student attributes and work habits. A counselor might assist the student in learning how to turn large assignments into smaller, more manageable pieces. In an extreme case, the teacher might require the student to complete their homework at school before going home. Teachers, along with as many as two or three other adults, tailor the specifics to the needs of each student. Regardless of the scenario, the team works to find the most relevant, targeted solution to the student's challenge, whether it's deadline struggles, disorganization, or a lack of efficient study habits.

If a student consistently doesn't complete work and refuses to participate in any intervention, then it becomes a disciplinary issue. Again, discipline is not code for removal and isolation; however, issues of discipline cannot go unchecked. Schools have already established expected social norms for good behavior and respectful interactions, so if the student violates these, the response should align with any established disciplinary procedures. Student age also is a factor in determining the response to inappropriate behavior. That said, remember that what looks like apathy may be a lack of understanding or increased anxiety. Be cautious in responding too swiftly from a disciplinary perspective. The line between can't dos and didn't dos can blur at times, so when in doubt, teachers should assume it's a can't-do situation until they confirm that it really is a didn't-do one.

Summary

Exclusionary approaches to discipline do not work; they are not instructional, they typically leave students feeling socially isolated, and they rarely lead to improved outcomes and social skills. While consequences (punishments) for behavioral transgressions may be readily accepted by society as a whole, they often turn the student-teacher relationship into an unwinnable power struggle. There is too much research and collective professional expertise in the 21st century for schools to continue to respond to antisocial behaviors like it's 1981.

The underpinnings of an effective approach to school discipline are to be trauma informed and to be restorative. By assuming all students have experienced some trauma, educators will develop a plan that accounts for students' potential for rapid emotional escalation. And by looking at discipline through a restorative lens, educators will recognize that the alarm and fear mental states will have students thinking emotionally, which could lead to regrettable responses from both the students and the educators. Maintaining a restorative lens also means that even when there are behavioral missteps (and there will be), educators remain fixated on restoring the relationships to the point where students authentically believe that, despite their missteps, they remain integral parts of the school community.

To achieve this, schools need a plan that creates predictability for the students, families, and educators alike. Having a system in place that makes it clear how responsibilities are distributed (at least initially) goes a long way to tamping down the impact raw emotions can have on decision making. The system should be fair and reasonable and have an undercurrent of open communication about what happened, what's next, and how we prevent future incidents.

But students and the circumstances that emerge from antisocial behaviors are not monolithic, so it is essential that schools make finite distinctions between those students who have a skill deficiency (can't do) and those who, for various reasons, simply did not follow through on their responsibility (didn't do). As well, preplanning for error frequency (infrequent versus chronic) prevents over- or underreaction to the situation at hand. Classroom teachers always have the opportunity to work outside the established guidelines when there is consensus that the student and the situation warrant it; however, without a plan, a school's approach to student discipline is likely to be haphazard and arbitrary.

Questions for Learning Teams

1. What quotation or passage encapsulates your main takeaway from this chapter? What immediate action (small, medium, or large) will you take as a result of this takeaway? Explain both to your team.

2. Generally speaking, would you describe your school's approach to displays of antisocial student behavior as one of *discipline* or one of *punishment*? What evidence do you have to support your assertion?

3. To what degree has your school's approach to discipline been *trauma informed* (guided by the overarching goal of keeping students in calm and alert mental states, regardless of how severe their antisocial behavior is)? What aspects of strength and aspects in need of strengthening do you recognize?

4. How intentionally restorative is your school's approach to discipline? Does your school use a predictable system or process to restore relationships and prevent students from feeling alienated (maybe even permanently) from the school content?

5. Does your school have a clear system that distinguishes office- versus classroom-managed antisocial behaviors? If so, how successful do you think it has been in creating a culture that is predictable for both students (they know how the adults will respond) and educators (they are clear on the process and progression of action)?

6. Generally speaking, do you think most educators in your school still view academic missteps as can't-do issues and behavioral missteps as didn't-do issues? What steps can be taken to permanently shift this mindset so educators prioritize behavioral instruction over behavioral consequences?

CHAPTER 6

Prioritizing and Reporting on Behavioral Attributes

By reporting non-cognitive aspects of students' performance separately on report cards and transcripts, educators make them "count" even more than they did in more traditional forms of reporting.

—THOMAS R. GUSKEY

In the insular world of education, it is easy to become dismissive of report cards or reporting systems, but educators are not the only ones who use the information these reports provide. Parents and families, of course, are the primary consumers of any reporting system; however, school districts, regional consortia, states, provinces, colleges, universities, and others also rely on this information for various decision-making processes. Admittedly, what is reported tends to mostly center on academic achievement, but there is no reason that schools and districts can't also report on students' social competence.

While many schools have some behavioral indicators via work habits or citizenship ratings, educators lament the fact that students and parents don't take behavioral attributes seriously. The answer is not to eliminate them but to enhance them by working with students and families from a reporting perspective. If behavioral attributes appear on the report card (or some kind of formal report), it is likely that students and parents (or at least more of them) will take them seriously.

Prioritizing Behavioral Accountability

As educators, we can't say that students need to learn to be more responsible and then not put any time and effort into formally reporting on the students' levels of responsibility. We have to prioritize behavioral accountability, and there are no better indicators of prioritization than time and attention.

Time and Attention

A number of years ago, I was working with a school in Southern California when an Advanced Placement (AP) English literature teacher, Alecia, shared with me a conversation she had with her students. The conversation was about repurposing homework as a formative exercise that emphasized practice over performance. Rather than grading the homework assignments, the school was focusing on advancing the students' learning through feedback. This was part of the school's overall effort to implement sounder and more accurate grading practices. While this shift in emphasis had energized Alecia and many of her colleagues, they were running into a bit of a challenge.

The challenge was twofold. First, not every teacher had embraced this new paradigm of practice, which meant that in some classes, homework was still graded. The students were choosing to spend more time on the assignments that were graded and, therefore, inconsistently (or not at all) completing the assignments that were for practice. This, of course, frustrated Alecia (and some of her colleagues), so she spoke to her AP students about this one day and dug a little deeper. What emerged from the meeting was unexpected and revealed an inadvertent influence that teachers had on the students' mindsets.

Alecia asked her students why they always chose to spend more time on the graded homework than the nongraded homework. The conversation was relatively frustrating for Alecia since she couldn't get a straight answer from her students. She finally pressed the students on why they didn't invest more in the learning for the classes where homework was not graded. After a long pause, a student near the back of the room raised his hand and said to Alecia, "The reason we focus on the graded assignments, and the reason why we are all so grade obsessed, is because that's all our teachers ever talk about—grades." For Alecia, this brought about an immediate paradigm shift. Many teachers in her school cynically believed that the students were just "grade grubbers" who had no interest in learning; they didn't realize the students were that way primarily because of what the teachers gave their attention to.

What educators give their attention to is what students will come to believe is important. Giving time and attention to behavioral accountability begins with the adults prioritizing responsibility and other behavioral attributes. Educators can pontificate for hours about how important behavioral characteristics are, but the proof is how much time and attention (not oxygen) they commit to developing, assessing, and reporting on these skills. It is hypocritical to say, "We teach more than just the curriculum; we teach the whole student," but then, when faced with actually making a concerted effort to prioritize those other attributes, to say, "Oh, we don't have time for that. There are too many standards to cover." Educators can't have it both ways.

So much of the focus on student attributes in schools happens on an ad hoc basis. Most teachers address behavioral attributes when issues or missteps arise, and teachers typically do an effective job of redirecting most students to more prosocial behaviors. It's important to acknowledge that is happening. However, being *reactive* means nothing is purposeful or prioritized. Going from good to great requires prioritization, proactivity, and commitment that are as serious and intentional as the development of academic skills. Schools unwilling to commit the necessary time and attention to teaching, assessing, and reporting must refrain from expressing any frustration with the limited or lack of social competence shown by their students.

Reporting

Change doesn't have to mean doing something completely different. Sometimes, educators can take advantage of existing structures and processes to prioritize responsibility and other important behavioral attributes, and there is no more entrenched structure in schools than the report card. Whether still in a tangible form or modernized through electronic access, the report card is a mainstay of the education system. Yes, report cards have gone through many iterations, but what hasn't changed is the importance that parents and others place on these periodic updates on student achievement and progress. A robust debate about the relevance of report cards is long overdue, but that's a conversation for another book. Even if an overhaul of this reporting system were accomplished, the need to report student achievement to families and others would remain, so educators should have behavioral attributes appear on report cards. Nothing will send a stronger message to students, families, and other stakeholders that student attributes *also* matter than this will.

Where behavior ratings appear on the report card matters; it can also send a strong message about student attributes' importance. In elementary schools where students spend the majority of their day with one teacher, the attributes could be reported at or near the top of the report card, akin to where a newspaper or website headline appears. The most important stories always appear *above the fold*, and reporting attributes at the top communicates that the development of these attributes is important. In middle and high schools where students have many different teachers who see them for only finite periods, the reporting would more likely occur on a subject-by-subject basis (for example, What is the student's level of responsibility in science?) or through some hybrid method that mirrors the homeroom or core-subject structure. Where and how to report on behavior is a school-based decision and would likely reflect the school's master schedule.

Taking advantage of the existing report card structure can be effective; however, some educators worry that if behavioral attributes are mixed with achievement grades, behavioral attributes will be marginalized as students and parents prioritize achievement grades. To combat this, schools may also consider a completely different reporting structure for behavioral attributes that occurs at intervals between the academic reporting. For example, if a school's academic reporting happens on a quarterly basis, then the school might report on student attributes on a trimester basis to avoid overlap. Figure 6.1 illustrates what a schedule could look like.

SEMESTER 1				
August	**September**	**October**	**November**	**December**
	Student Behavioral Attribute Reporting	Quarter 1 Academic Report Card		Quarter 2 Academic Report Card
SEMESTER 2				
January	**February**	**March**	**April**	**May**
Student Behavioral Attribute Reporting		Quarter 3 Academic Report Card	Student Behavioral Attribute Reporting	Quarter 4 Academic Report Card

Figure 6.1: Separate behavioral attribute reporting schedule.

A potential downside of a separate reporting system is teachers could perpetually feel as if they are on the cusp of yet another report card period. A potential upside would be the time, focus, and energy that students, families, and even educators themselves could give to behavioral attributes since the efforts to develop, nurture, and sustain these attributes will be intentional rather than haphazard. Each school is free to make the decision that best suits it and its community, so there really is no wrong decision in the abstract. A decision would be wrong only if it were ill-suited for the school community.

The Sweet Spot

If you've ever picked up your vehicle from a mechanic who launched into a step-by-step, detailed description of how your vehicle was repaired, then you understand the notion of too much detail. Simply hearing the vehicle is fixed with little to no detail is usually not enough for most people, but that doesn't mean those same people want a ten-minute presentation on the repair process. While students are more important and complex than vehicles, the principles of efficiency and effectiveness still hold true for reporting on students: there should be enough detail to effectively report on the students, but parents and families should also be able to efficiently consume the reports.

Whether reporting academic achievement or student behavioral attributes, schools have to find the sweet spot between providing too much information and providing too little information for each student. This is where contextual norms and expectations will have to be considered. Parents and families are busy. Educators should not view families as apathetic toward their children's education simply because they don't necessarily have time to read extensive reports. While there might be apathetic parents and families, most parents and families care deeply about how their children are developing both the academic skills and the behavioral attributes that lead to success in life.

If parents and families have had access to the tools and information the school uses to teach, acknowledge, and reinforce the behavioral attributes, then the reports themselves need not be lengthy; they can simply be a rating that references what parents and families are already familiar with. The less access to and interaction with the supporting materials parents and families have, the more details schools should consider providing on behavioral attributes. Each school will have to decide on this within the context of its unique school community since what constitutes too much or too little detail will likely vary.

Rating Student Attributes

While there are assessment fundamentals that remain whether reporting academic achievement or behavioral attributes, schools have some choices to make when designing their system of rating and reporting.

Frequency Scale

Most student behavioral attributes are binary; for example, there are not several versions of quality for meeting a deadline. The student either met the deadline or did not meet it. The student either was respectful or was disrespectful. Therefore, the most effective choice when addressing binary skills or habits (and binary academic standards) is to rate *frequency*—the frequency or consistency with which the student meets deadlines, is respectful, is self-directed, and so on. Does the student, for example, *consistently*, *usually*, *sometimes*, or *rarely* act responsibly?

It is possible to conceptualize levels of quality on some attributes. For example, one can imagine levels of disrespect since interrupting someone is probably seen differently than verbally disparaging someone is. However, for the sake of clarity and simplicity, schools would be wise to stick with a frequency scale since most attributes are binary and the mixing of frequency and quality within a reporting system may be confusing. Conversations with students about levels of quality are more likely well timed during instruction as the specifics of each attribute are taught, developed, reinforced, and sustained.

The one level schools must avoid is *always*, as in, "The student is always responsible." The majority of adults can't live up to the *always* expectation, so it is unreasonable to expect students to. Everyone makes mistakes, and the *always* rating provides no leeway or flexibility for a momentary lapse in judgment or an unintentional misstep. Similar to the *exceeds expectations* label for academic achievement, *always* creates an unreasonable expectation of perfection, which no human being can attain.

Number of Levels

Research indicates that limiting levels to a few clearly discernible ones leads to reliability (Brookhart & Guskey, 2019), but this research stops short of dictating the exact number of levels. While this research focuses on the consistency with which teachers make indirect scoring inferences about academic performance, common sense would suggest that the same holds true for student behavioral attributes and social competence. After all, teachers will still be making indirect inferences about the frequency with which students have demonstrated the attributes that serve as the schoolwide focus.

Some might lean toward ensuring the same number of levels for both academic achievement and social competence, but there is no research that asserts this is necessary. The necessity is that educators can clearly distinguish each level of performance. The American Community School of Abu Dhabi in the United Arab Emirates, for example, has four academic levels (1 to 4) but only three levels for what it refers to as its *approaches to learning* (consistently, sometimes, and rarely). Whether your school chooses to use the same symbols for both (for example, numbers) or different symbols (numbers for academic achievement and letters for student attributes) is a local decision. Schools should take into consideration what educators and parents and families can reasonably distinguish between. The argument for using different symbols to make the reporting of achievement and behavioral attributes clearer to students, parents, families, and others is strong; however, if schools suspect this or any other system will inhibit people from easily consuming what's being reported, they would be wise to avoid it.

Calibration

Admittedly, the concept of frequency can be open to interpretation (What exactly does *consistently* or *sometimes* mean?). This is why schools must have collaborative conversations to ensure alignment among teachers who are determining frequency. Reliability is important so schools can make valid interpretations of what teachers are observing, determining, and reporting about student behavior and so schools can gauge the strength of their schoolwide efforts to teach and develop behavioral attributes.

Alignment, not uniformity, is the likely outcome of calibration efforts. One can expect there to be some nuanced differences on single observations of students; however, as a body of evidence grows (meaning observations over time), and given that there are only a few choices, the consistency with which teachers determine students' levels of behavioral competence will increase. The key is that conversation among teachers about the success criteria should ensure that they are all on the same page in terms of what they *name* and *notice*; The principles of sound assessment practices still hold regardless of what's being assessed.

Since assessment of student behavioral attributes is mostly interactive and observational, the calibration becomes that much more important. When calibrating academic achievement criteria, teachers can share student samples with their colleagues, but teachers are likely unable to bring student behavioral samples to team meetings. The descriptions of what teachers observe will be critical. The calibration, again, is focused on the few attributes (like respect and responsibility) that serve as the schoolwide focus. Any other attributes (such as work ethic) a teacher or a small group of teachers may be addressing will unlikely get the same time and attention in terms of collective conversations.

Reporting on Behavioral Attributes

Reporting on responsibility and other behavioral attributes is actually quite straightforward. The heavy lifting is in the setup; establishing the criteria, teaching students to meet those criteria, and informing everyone within the school community of the instructional process will make reporting seamless and relatively simple. Following are some examples from elementary, middle, and high schools. Schools are limited only by their collective imagination of what best suits their context.

Elementary Schools

Since elementary school students spend most of the day with one teacher, attributes tend to be reported separately from academic achievement. It would be repetitive for an elementary teacher to duplicate the ratings for each subject because students typically remain in a single classroom.

Figure 6.2 illustrates the format an elementary school might use to report the designated student behavioral attributes (habits of learning).

HABITS OF LEARNING	Quarter 1	Quarter 2	Quarter 3	Quarter 4
Responsible: Student is answerable for their actions.				
Respectful: Student shows self-regard and regard for others.				
Self-directed: Student takes charge of their own learning.				
Collaborative: Student contributes to the learning of others.				
Comments:				

Key: **C** = Consistently, **U** = Usually, **S** = Sometimes, **R** = Rarely

Figure 6.2: Example elementary school format for behavioral attribute reporting.

Figure 6.2 assumes a quarterly reporting system; the presence of all four quarters on each report card allows for the longitudinal tracking of growth or the identification of fluctuations throughout the school year. Having a space for comments at the elementary level helps the primary teacher provide context to the ratings. As elementary students are in the early stages of their school experience, being able to substantiate and contextualize the ratings will help parents make sense of how the teacher determined them.

At the same time, an abundance of comments (or unfocused comments) can become overwhelming. Taking the 3–2–1 approach can help avoid overwhelming feelings. This approach entails commenting on three specific aspects of strength, two aspects in need of strengthening, and one way that parents can support their child's growth toward social competence. Of course, teachers *can* provide more information than six sentences' worth, but it is important to be aware of the overall length of the comment section, which can become very long, especially if academic subjects are also featured.

Middle Schools

Middle schools could adopt the elementary school format since some middle schools have their students spend the majority of their day with a single core teacher. However, if we assume some level of teaming (something more common in middle school), then we would adjust the reporting format to reflect the students' schedule.

Figure 6.3 (page 118) illustrates the format for a middle school assuming two core academic subjects are taught by one teacher. In this case, there is no need to duplicate the assessment of the behavioral habits of learning since the teacher is the same and students are unlikely to display markedly different levels of social competence in different subjects. Even if some did, the ratings could be thought of as hybrids or syntheses of the two classes. Schools, again, are free to add as much or as little detail as necessary to clearly communicate student competence.

If the schedule for a middle school has students with various teachers, then the school might mirror what high schools would likely do—each subject reporting the habits of learning separately. Where the same teacher teaches the student more than one subject, there may need to be some duplication of reporting within the report card.

MATHEMATICS	Quarter 1	Quarter 2	Quarter 3	Quarter 4
Ratios and Proportions				
The Number System				
Expressions and Equations				
Geometry				
Statistics and Probability				
Modeling With Mathematics				
Constructing Arguments and Critiquing Reasoning				
Perseverance in Problem Solving				

SCIENCE	Quarter 1	Quarter 2	Quarter 3	Quarter 4
Argument From Evidence				
Developing and Using Models				
Constructing Explanations and Designing Solutions				
Analyzing and Interpreting Data				
Using Mathematics and Computational Thinking				
Asking Questions and Defining Problems				
Planning and Carrying Out Investigations				
Obtaining and Communicating Information				

Mathematics Comments:

Science Comments:

HABITS OF LEARNING (Consistently, Usually, Sometimes, Rarely)	Quarter 1	Quarter 2	Quarter 3	Quarter 4
Responsible: Student is answerable for their actions.				
Respectful: Student shows self-regard and regard for others.				
Self-directed: Student takes charge of their own learning.				
Collaborative: Student contributes to the learning of others.				
Comments:				

Figure 6.3: Example middle school format for behavioral attribute reporting.

High Schools

The most likely scenario with high schools is that the habits of learning are reported within the context of each separate subject. While it is not uncommon for a student to have the same teacher for multiple subjects, it is certainly not the norm in most high schools. The separation does provide a contextual reference for ratings that may be helpful in connecting the students' academic success to their habits of learning.

A student with high achievement but poor habits of learning would likely be interpreted as having succeeded through already established skills or background knowledge; this student would need behavioral intervention to develop the habits of learning because background knowledge and skills are unlikely to be enough to succeed long term. On the other hand, a student with low achievement but high ratings on the habits of learning would likely be interpreted as someone with the desirable work ethic but in need of academic intervention since the achievement side is what needs addressing.

Figure 6.4 illustrates what a high school might do, assuming the habits of learning are reported for each subject. Once again, whether to add comments or details regarding the ratings is a district- or school-based decision, and starting with a degree of specificity (criteria and specific details of instruction for the habits of learning) will likely mean a more streamlined approach to reporting. High schools whose configuration mirrors that of a middle or even elementary school (for example, rural schools where the same teacher teaches multiple subjects) may choose to utilize an elementary or middle school type of reporting format since efficiency and effectiveness in reporting must be prioritized. Figure 6.4 shows an example for high school reporting.

Ensuring a Manageable Reporting System

As discussed previously, some schools and districts may choose to report on student attributes separately from the regular cycle of achievement reporting to ensure that student behavioral attributes receive the full attention they deserve. When choosing to do so, however, schools and districts should be cautious to contain this reporting (not flood teachers' workload) and be sure to involve students.

HABITS OF LEARNING	Quarter 1	Quarter 2	Quarter 3	Quarter 4
Reading				
Writing				
Speaking and Listening				
Language Development				
English Language Arts Comments:				
Academic Proficiency Scale: E = Exemplary, P = Proficient, D = Developing, N = Novice				
HABITS OF LEARNING	**Quarter 1**	**Quarter 2**	**Quarter 3**	**Quarter 4**
Responsible: Student is answerable for their actions.				
Respectful: Student shows self-regard and regard for others.				
Self-directed: Student takes charge of their own learning.				
Collaborative: Student contributes to the learning of others.				
Habits of Learning Comments:				
Habits of Learning Rating Scale: C = Consistently, U = Usually, S = Sometimes, R = Rarely				

Figure 6.4: Example high school format for behavioral attribute reporting.

Keep It Contained

While separating student attribute reporting from academic achievement reporting has many advantages, schools and districts would be wise to contain the effort so as to not disproportionately increase teacher workload. The separation will bring an increased focus from students and families, but it can also inadvertently create a situation where teachers are in a constant state of reporting or preparing to report.

One way to contain the effort is to implement a protocol that intentionally restricts the number of comments permitted; this will do two things. First, it will create a guardrail for the workload issue. While managing the workload is not the primary concern, it has to be *a* concern so that the effort does not look (or feel) like just another add-on to what teachers already have to do. Second, it will force teachers to report on that which is most pressing—to be specific about a student's strengths and aspects in need of strengthening.

Figure 6.5 shows what a separate report could look like. The combination of a rating scale and specific comments about strengths and aspects in need of strengthening provides the right balance for a separate reporting schedule to give more, but not too much, detail. By predetermining that there will be only six comments (3–2–1), teachers can balance their feedback. As well, schools might choose to include a comment about how families can support the students' continued growth in the attributes, thereby creating another link between what is being taught and developed at school and how that learning and support can continue at home.

Involve Students

Another way to manage the workload is to distribute it by turning the reporting of student attributes into a student-driven exercise; this is something we will explore more extensively in chapter 7 (page 127). If the reporting on attributes is anchored in students' assessing themselves and increasingly regulating their own growth and development, not only will there be less work for teachers to do, but students will also learn to be self-regulatory and be in a position to determine their next steps.

The benefits of student self- and peer assessment are well established (Brown & Harris, 2013; Karaman, 2021; Topping, 2013), but these processes don't seamlessly happen overnight. The processes and practices of self-assessment (and especially peer assessment) have to be intentionally taught so that they don't regress into pointless exercises of platitudes or unhelpful criticisms. The easy part is to envision what a student-centered process might look like; the great challenge is to purposefully and methodically bring that student-centered norm to fruition. Once we create the norms and expectations of excellence with student attributes, the next step is to turn the process over to students and have them drive it.

HABITS OF LEARNING	Quarter 1	Quarter 2	Quarter 3	Quarter 4
Responsible: Student is answerable for their actions.				
Respectful: Student shows self-regard and regard for others.				
Self-directed: Student takes charge of their own learning.				
Collaborative: Student contributes to the learning of others.				

Three specific aspects of strength:

1.

2.

3.

Two specific aspects in need of strengthening:

1.

2.

One specific way to support growth from home:

1.

Key: C = Consistently, **U** = Usually, **S** = Sometimes, **R** = Rarely

Figure 6.5: Stand-alone reporting example for behavioral attributes.

Summary

Students learn what matters more from what educators do than from what they say. Giving time and attention to developing student attributes will send a clear signal that these attributes matter. There is no stronger signal than including student attributes within the report card.

The reporting of student attributes will be slightly different from for the reporting of academic achievement. While academic achievement is typically reported on a scale that emphasizes quality, student attributes are more effectively reported on a frequency scale since most attributes are binary—the student either did or did not act in a prosocial manner. Consistency in action is how positive behavioral attributes will become habitual. For teachers, it is essential to spend some time calibrating their interpretations of each of the ratings with their colleagues so there is alignment in how they observe and assess students.

A school or district must decide how it wants to structure the reporting process. Schools will need to find the sweet spot between reporting too much information and not enough. Including the most information possible might sound desirable, but schools should take care not to overload teachers or confuse parents and families with the process. If schools make the criteria for behavioral expectations, the instructional process, examples, feedback, and so on clear and transparent for students and families, then the actual reporting (on a report card or a separate report) can be more streamlined. Educators are limited only by their imaginations when it comes to reporting student attributes, but they must be mindful of striking the right balance so that the reporting is substantive (effective) yet easily consumable (efficient).

Questions for Learning Teams

1. What quotation or passage encapsulates your main takeaway from this chapter? What immediate action (small, medium, or large) will you take as a result of this takeaway? Explain both to your team.

2. Is there a difference between how educators in your school talk about student attributes and the amount of time and attention educators are prepared to dedicate to teaching and reporting on student attributes?

3. How seriously do you think students and families take student attributes as an important aspect of the overall school experience (seriously, somewhat seriously, or not seriously)? If you answered *somewhat seriously* or *not seriously*, then explain why you think that is and what can be done to reconcile that.

4. What existing reporting systems and structures in your school could you capitalize on to seamlessly transition to a more robust reporting system?

5. What would your sweet spot be for reporting on student attributes? Explain.

6. Do you think there is an appetite for a reporting system that addresses student attributes separately from academic achievement? Why or why not?

CHAPTER 7

Self-Regulating Student Accountability

Children and youth need to develop skills that enable self-regulation and dispositions that support self-efficacy and social contribution.

— LINDA DARLING-HAMMOND

The irony of implementing all the systems, structures, practices, and processes needed to redefine accountability and bring student behavioral attributes to the forefront is that the ultimate goal is to not need any of them. The goal is for student social competence to be so strong that minimal to no adult monitoring is necessary. What is likely to begin as a teacher-centered process must lead to a self-regulatory approach where students monitor and report on their own progress to become independent and efficacious learners.

Social-Emotional Learning

With purposeful attention and effort, specific social-skill development can blossom under the umbrella of social-emotional learning competencies that lay a foundation for students to become self-reliant, reflective people, not just students.

What SEL Is

There is broad agreement that teachers need to teach more than just the academic standards. Social development also matters so that as members of a society, students can interact skillfully and respectfully with the people in their lives, maintain healthy mental states, and develop habits and dispositions that leave them poised for success in whatever they do. Students' developmental characteristics (cognitive, social, language, emotional, and physical) are interwoven, making it essential that schools attend to all these developmental characteristics (Aksoy & Gresham, 2020). The COVID-19 pandemic magnified the need for educators to pay close attention to the whole child as the stress and pressure that students and their families felt in all aspects of their lives were (and in many ways still are) relentless. Even prior to the COVID-19 pandemic, Linda Darling-Hammond (2015) asserted, "Attending to students' psychological needs is as much a part of a quality education as ensuring that they have adequate resources, good instructional materials, and well-trained teachers" (p. xi). If that was true then, imagine how true it is in the wake of the pandemic.

SEL involves implementing practices that help students acquire and apply the knowledge, skills, and attitudes that can enhance their personal development and their interpersonal relationships (Weissberg, Durlak, Domitrovich, & Gullotta, 2015). Through the combination of direct instruction and student-centered learning, students develop *social* and *emotional* competence. Though not exclusive to school-age children (SEL is essential for adults too), school-based SEL efforts focus on bringing a *wholeness* to the educational experience. The principles of SEL are fairly ubiquitous, but each unique approach to SEL differs in which specific content it includes, how it presents that content, and how it sustains high-quality presentation of that content over time (Brackett, Elbertson, & Rivers, 2015). The *content* refers to the specific social skills and strategies that allow students to understand and manage their emotions so that healthy, productive relationships with both themselves and others can emerge. There will, of course, be plenty of overlap between schools, but each school would be wise to consider its unique context.

SEL was first introduced in the 1990s as an amalgamation of ideas from researchers, educators, and advocates (Brackett et al., 2015). In a blog post for the Committee for Children, Kim Gulbrandson (2019) writes about several significant findings in the SEL research. According to Gulbrandson (2019), one study (Durlak, Weissberg,

Dymnicki, Taylor, & Schellinger, 2011) "propelled the SEL–academic connection to the forefront." Joseph A. Durlak and colleagues' (2011) meta-analysis notes that "students participating in these universal SEL programs . . . showed an 11-percentile-point gain in achievement, suggesting that SEL may strengthen academic success" (Gulbrandson, 2019).

Other findings that Gulbrandson (2019) cites include the positive long-term effects of SEL programs as protective factors against later conduct problems, emotional distress, and drug use. Gulbrandson's (2019) closing paragraph sums up the emerging research in SEL quite well:

> The evolving research is indicating that social-emotional learning supports provide students with skills that both promote well-being and protect against negative outcomes. Although SEL is not a one-size-fits-all approach, it's an effective strategy regardless of school location and socioeconomic status. Students and teachers report the benefits of SEL, and teachers affect SEL outcomes. There are also both economic and long-term benefits of SEL programming.

The benefits reach beyond the social and emotional, as it is becoming clear that children's interactions with their environments impact various biological systems, including their immune system, cardiovascular system, endocrine system, and brain (Greenberg, Katz, & Klein, 2015). Environmental stress can interfere with a child's social, cognitive, and physical development.

The CASEL Framework

The Collaborative for Academic, Social, and Emotional Learning has established a comprehensive model that helps cultivate skills and environments that advance student learning and development. The *CASEL 5* or *wheel* addresses five broad, interrelated areas of competence: (1) self-awareness, (2) self-management, (3) social awareness, (4) relationship skills, and (5) responsible decision making. According to CASEL (n.d.b), these five areas:

> can be taught and applied at various developmental stages from childhood to adulthood and across diverse cultural contexts . . . [to] articulate what students should know and be able to do for academic success, school and civic engagement, health and wellness, and fulfilling careers.

In addition to the five SEL competencies, the framework makes clear the need for an integrated approach both within the school (classwide and schoolwide) and among the school, families, and the community at large.

At the heart of the CASEL framework are the five competencies that emphasize the importance of internal and external competence so students can develop healthy identities, maintain healthy relationships, and make responsible decisions. Following is an abridged version of the CASEL 5 competencies; readers are encouraged to go directly to the CASEL website (https://casel.org) for a more detailed version of the framework:

- **Self-awareness:** The abilities to understand one's own emotions, thoughts, and values and how they influence behavior across contexts

- **Self-management:** The abilities to manage one's emotions, thoughts, and behaviors effectively in different situations and to achieve goals and aspirations

- **Social awareness:** The abilities to understand the perspectives of and empathize with others, including those from diverse backgrounds, cultures, and contexts

- **Relationship skills:** The abilities to establish and maintain healthy and supportive relationships and to effectively navigate settings with diverse individuals and groups

- **Responsible decision making:** The abilities to make caring and constructive choices about personal behavior and social interactions across diverse situations (CASEL, n.d.b)

What is clear, considering the primary purpose of this book, is that redefining student accountability falls squarely within the CASEL framework (responsible decision making), as do other essential student attributes schools can and do focus on.

The SAFE Approach

SEL researcher Roger Weissberg and his colleagues (2015) submit that effective approaches to SEL often incorporate four elements represented by the acronym *SAFE*: (1) *sequenced* (making a connected and coordinated effort to develop SEL skills), (2) *active* (having students actively learn new skills), (3) *focused* (developing both personal and social skills), and (4) *explicit* (targeting specific social and emotional skills). They add that the inclusion of the word *learning* in "social-emotional learning" is intentional. This word reflects that the SEL competencies can be taught and that schools are a primary place within which children and adolescents can learn them (Weissberg et al., 2015).

The theme of intentionality underpins this book; if we educators want it, we teach it. Rather than leaving things to chance, we must intentionally teach social skills and ultimately the SEL competencies because this is paramount to all students' success in growing holistically as learners and as social beings.

Ends, Not Means

The five CASEL competencies represent desirable default behavioral dispositions that need to be taught; students will not automatically self-manage without intentional and sustained effort. Positioning SEL competencies as ends rather than means will create clear and obvious goals for students and will ensure that educators create a purposeful instructional plan that not only reshapes the environment but also has the self-regulation of these competencies as the essential outcome.

When the SEL competencies are viewed as the *ends* (the goals), then specific social skills and dispositions can be positioned as the *means* (the ways to achieve the goals). In other words, the SEL competencies are viewed as a collection of specific social skills and dispositions. Being a responsible decision maker will include managing and meeting deadlines, and it will also more broadly include making decisions about things such as potential solutions to personal or social dilemmas, the benefits and drawbacks of interpersonal relationships, and their role in their own (and the collective) well-being. Thinking of the five SEL competencies as five overlapping umbrellas provides a structure and focus to the day-to-day social-skill instruction.

Positioning the SEL competencies as ends also creates clarity for the evolution of the model itself. Most schools, when trying to establish or reinvigorate a focus on social competence, will turn to a PBIS model that is teacher centered and explicit about specific social-skill instruction. On one end of the social competence continuum, there are schools that already have a low number of antisocial incidents, so they may seamlessly and immediately immerse themselves in reflective activities surrounding the SEL competencies. On the other end, there are schools that face a relentless onslaught of behaviors that violate established social norms, so they are likely to be more granular with establishing and maintaining specific prosocial norms within the school. Other schools will find themselves somewhere along the continuum between those two extremes, so each school will have its own unique entry point.

A Venn diagram (figure 7.1, page 132) of the PBIS model and the CASEL framework provides a big picture that schools can establish to purposefully transfer management to students. Because it includes self-awareness and self-management as two of the five SEL competencies, the student-centered, self-regulatory CASEL framework is perfectly suited to serving as the transition point away from the more adult-centered PBIS model. But this transition is unlikely to be an all-or-nothing proposition. It is reasonable to expect that the majority of students will eventually transfer to a self-regulatory model (success at Tier 1). Some students will likely need *occasional* adult monitoring (Tier 2). Still, there are likely to be a few who *consistently* need and benefit from more intensive adult monitoring (Tier 3). The gradual release of responsibility for monitoring from educators to students has to be the end goal of redefining accountability and the development of any aspects of social competence.

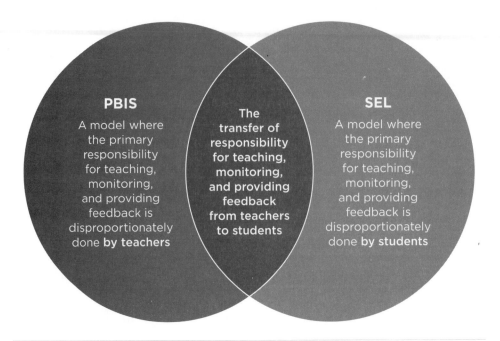

Figure 7.1: PBIS to SEL continuum.

Self-Assessment and Peer Assessment

While self-observation and self-management (strategies in response) are essential, it is also essential that students have an accurate sense of self so they have the ability to self-assess. Additionally, sometimes students will come to see themselves more authentically through the eyes of peers, so facilitating peer assessment and feedback opportunities can also be advantageous to individual student growth. The transfer of responsibility for monitoring includes the transfer of responsibility for assessment.

Student Investment

Student investment is the desirable outcome of educators' establishing their expertise with sound assessment practices (Dimich, Erkens, & Schimmer, 2023). Educators' assessment expertise is what allows them to teach students how to assess themselves and their peers both academically and socially. My colleagues (Cassandra Erkens and Nicole Dimich) and I established an assessment framework anchored in six essential assessment tenets that are timeless and universally foundational to assessing anything (Erkens et al., 2017). Figure 7.2 illustrates the framework.

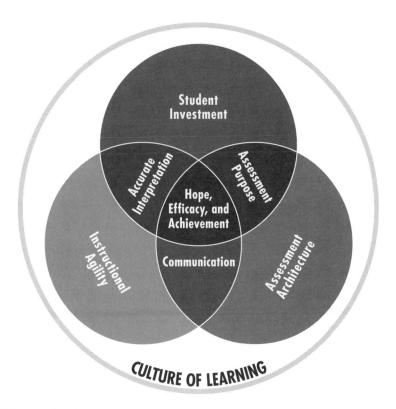

Source: Erkens et al., 2017.

Figure 7.2: Solution Tree Assessment Center's six essential assessment tenets.

The following list provides teachers with a brief description of each tenet (Erkens et al., 2017).

1. **Assessment purpose:** Understanding our assessment purpose means we have a clear picture of how we intend to use the emerging assessment results before the assessment.

2. **Assessment architecture:** Assessment is most effective when it is planned, purposeful, and intentionally designed and sequenced in advance of instruction by all those responsible for the delivery.

3. **Accurate interpretation:** The interpretation of assessment results must be accurate, accessible, and reliable. This means the items and tasks in our assessments must accurately reflect the standards we are gathering information on.

4. **Instructional agility:** Being instructionally agile means teachers have the capacity to use emerging evidence to make real-time modifications within the context of the expected learning.

5. **Communication:** The communication of assessment results must generate productive responses from learners and all stakeholders who support them.

6. **Student investment:** Learners must be able to track their progress and reflect on what they are learning and where they need to go next.

While the six tenets are interdependent and do not represent a definitive hierarchy of practice, my colleagues and I intentionally positioned student investment in the framework. We wanted educators to see student investment at the top of the illustrated framework as a way of inferring its importance.

Student investment does not happen haphazardly; rather, it results from purposeful effort and action with the other five assessment tenets. When it comes to the assessment of social skills and the broader SEL competencies, students must exemplify the following.

1. Students must know the ***purpose*** of their assessments. If *formative*, then the focus will likely be more granular or specific; if *summative*, then the focus will likely be more holistic.

2. Students must be specific on the ***architecture*** of the evidence that will reveal their social competence. Through goal setting, students can in advance identify opportunities and experiences that will reveal competence.

3. Students must be clear on the ***interpretation*** of their evidence by establishing performance indicators that align with the constructed or co-constructed criteria. Is students' understanding of the frequency scale similar to that of their teachers?

4. Students must anticipate opportunities to be ***instructionally agile*** by envisioning various outcomes of their actions. If things don't go as planned, in what ways can they reconcile the situation?

5. Students must be able to ***communicate*** their reflective findings as to their status and articulate what's next along their personal growth trajectory.

Assessment is the engine that drives the processes and practices that turn what could be a superficial effort to teach students and grow their social skills into a meaningful one. Embedding the fundamental assessment tenets throughout the social learning experiences is how the transfer from teacher centered to student centered will be achieved. For example, teaching students to recognize natural opportunities to demonstrate social skills (assessment architecture), to self-assess to determine any discrepancy between the desirable outcome and what was just self-observed (accurate interpretation), and to determine any next steps or make any necessary adjustments (instructional agility)—to name a few—are ways students can meaningfully assess themselves along their growth trajectories.

Self-Assessment

Self-assessment is an exercise in which students take inventory of their current status, examine it against a desired outcome, and determine for themselves what comes next. It really is about students giving themselves feedback. The strategies for self-assessment are not distinct from the strategies teachers use; who drives the process is the distinction. Self-assessment actions are carried out by the student rather than by the teacher. While some educators distinguish self-assessment from self-evaluation (the former being about feedback while the latter is about grading), others might suggest that self-assessment includes both, since grading *is* assessment and assessment is just the gathering of information about student learning.

Research finds that self-assessment is positive and leads to benefits for students, not the least of which is learning self-regulatory processes such as self-observation, self-judgment, and self-reaction (Brown & Harris, 2013). In education, sometimes what's in students' best interest and what best suits the teacher's workload management conflict. However, with effective self-assessment implementation, teachers can distribute the assessment workload among students, which leads to a beneficial outcome for the students; it's a win-win situation.

Pinar Karaman's (2021) meta-analysis of self-assessment's impact on student performance supports the consensus on this positive impact. Specifically, Karaman's investigation finds two things are most helpful for transferring the self-assessment of responsibility and other attributes. The first is purposeful instruction before implementation. Karaman (2021) writes, "There are research studies suggesting that self-assessment training for students before self-assessment interventions contributed to increase effectiveness of self-assessment, self-regulated learning, and academic performance" (p. 1152). While students will be immersed in the criteria through the instructional process, this training would include teaching students how to assess their overall level of competence using the tools that were constructed or co-constructed.

The second useful finding is the important role of external feedback to ensure the accuracy of student self-assessments. Inaccurate self-assessment is counterproductive, so while Karaman (2021) submits that self-assessment without external feedback is more common, she finds that because "self-assessment is crucial for self-regulated learning, feedback is necessary for the accuracy of this assessment" (p. 1152). If students are going to accurately identify their next steps in growth toward either academic or social competence, ensuring the information they are basing those decisions on will be paramount. Though studies of external feedback's effect on self-assessment are limited, verifying the accuracy of self-assessments through external peer or teacher feedback is still a promising practice.

Age and ability are two important factors to be mindful of during the self-assessment process. In the *SAGE Handbook of Research on Classroom Assessment*, Gavin T. L. Brown and Lois R. Harris (2013) find that "empirical data show that age and proficiency are a powerful basis for more accurate self-evaluation" (p. 385). The older a student is, the more accurate their self-assessments tend to be, though Brown and Harris (2013) state it is not entirely clear whether accuracy is the direct result of age or increased school experience, as these tend to be synonymous. As well, the evidence that increased ability or competence is linked to increased accuracy in self-assessment is compelling. This matters because teachers need to set reasonable expectations for their students' accuracy in self-assessing given their relative age and competence.

Peer Assessment

Peer assessment can also have positive practical and educational impacts for both the teacher and the students. For the teacher, peer assessment allows for the distribution of the workload of providing feedback. Workload is not the number-one driver of a strategy, however. A benefit of peer assessment is that it creates a more active classroom by adding a social element nonexistent in self-assessment. Students need to learn how to assess performance (in this case, that of a peer) and also how to productively communicate their assessments to their peers. The social interaction and collaborative nature of peer assessment make it a multidimensional experience that has both benefits and potential detriments.

An upside of peer assessment and feedback is that it is more readily available than teacher feedback; there are simply more students than teachers in any classroom. According to researcher Keith J. Topping (2013), "Peer assessment of learning and social behavior sharpens and broadens the assessor's capabilities and relates to the processes of learning more than the products" (p. 396). In other words, as a student assesses their peers' competence, it positively impacts their own capabilities as well. The ability to recognize the competence in others sharpens students' ability to recognize competence in themselves. One way teachers could create these opportunities for peer assessment is through role playing. When students act out different scenarios, their peers can provide feedback and possible next steps for greater success. Obviously, there would also be real-time opportunities day to day, but teachers would be wise to remind students that impromptu, unsolicited feedback might not always be well received. The day-to-day opportunities that could arise (such as planning for a big project) are likely most effective when teacher guided.

Of course, a potential downside is that peers are not as expert as their teacher, so the feedback could be less accurate or less productive. There is an art to feedback that results in productive student responses (Erkens et al., 2017; Kluger & DeNisi, 1996). In addition, training is often required to implement peer assessment in the classroom (Thienpermpool, 2021). Students will need training from teachers on how to provide constructive feedback to peers as well as how to recognize productive interactions with peers. Making model demonstrations or dispositions available through criteria and examples increases the accuracy of peer assessment (Topping, 2013).

It is noteworthy that all five SEL competencies of the CASEL framework are authentically present in a collaborative peer assessment experience.

1. **Self-awareness:** Students will benefit from metacognitive awareness of how their thoughts and emotions are influencing how they interact with others.

2. **Self-management:** Students need to manage their emotions, thoughts, and behaviors, especially if feedback from peers is less than favorable.

3. **Social awareness:** The inherently social experience means students must be able to understand the perspectives of and empathize with others to optimize the collective gain.

4. **Relationship skills:** Students need to keep an eye on the long-term residual effects of consistent peer assessment opportunities; relationships must be protected and nurtured through the process.

5. **Responsible decision making:** Students need to make caring and constructive choices about personal actions and provide caring and constructive peer feedback.

Not only does peer assessment benefit each learner's growth toward an academic or behavioral goal, but it also gives students an inherent opportunity to practice the skills and processes they are developing. This does not mean the pathway to SEL competence is exclusively through peer assessment; it's not. Peer assessment is, however, a significant process to add to the totality of the experiences utilized in service of SEL.

Self-Regulation Through Assessment

The assessment cycle and the self-regulation of learning are perfectly aligned to support each other as simultaneous processes. Rather than being *if-then* linear processes, each can serve the other in a symbiotic relationship.

The Symbiotic Relationship

According to Michelle M. Robbins, Grace Onodipe, and Alan Marks (2020), the research on self-regulation has produced three overarching findings:

> First, self-regulation requires self-awareness, motivation, and the ability to implement behavioral change. . . . Second, self-regulation is a process of setting goals, implementing strategies, monitoring progress, making changes, managing time, and engaging in ongoing self-evaluation. . . . Finally, self-regulation requires self-motivation, which is linked to both intrinsic interest and self-efficacy in learning and mastering the material. (p. 21)

The second finding—the setting of goals and so on—is the epitome of a comprehensive assessment cycle that is active before, during, and after the learning.

D. Royce Sadler (1989) describes a theory of formative assessment that has long served as a model for others to articulate the cycle of assessment. Sadler asserts that in order for students to monitor their own learning, they must understand the learning goal, be able to compare their current performance with the learning goal, and take action to close the gap. Sadler (1989) synthesizes this into three guiding questions: (1) Where am I going? (2) Where am I now? and (3) How do I close the gap? These questions are ubiquitous among educators who are familiar with the processes associated with the formative assessment cycle. Others (Black & Wiliam, 1998; Chappuis, 2014; Hattie & Timperley, 2007) have used this foundational three-part framework in their own writings. The three guiding questions (and their many iterations) are the perfect inputs for students to be self-regulatory as they set their sights on an outcome, determine where they are in relation to that outcome, and identify next steps toward reaching that outcome.

Not only does assessment serve as an input for self-regulation, but it also serves as an output. Students who engage in self-regulatory activities show improved academic achievement. According to Brookhart (2013), "Self-regulation strategies and capabilities, or the lack of them, may be the defining feature that separates successful and unsuccessful students" (p. 43). This finding is true whether success is defined academically (Lawrence & Saileela, 2019) or behaviorally (Kaya, 2020). Rather than each being an *if-then* linear progression, self-regulation and assessment have a symbiotic relationship where each feeds the other, and simultaneously, each is positively impacted.

The Phases of Self-Regulation

While there are various self-regulatory models in the field, viewing the self-regulatory process as having cyclical phases that happen before, during, and after the learning helps to highlight the symbiotic relationship. Some advocate four phases (Pintrich & Zusho, 2002; Winne, 2011), while a three-phase model (where the middle two phases are simply synthesized) provides a more seamless connection to Sadler's (1989) three assessment questions.

Self-regulation expert Barry J. Zimmerman (2011) conceptualizes the self-regulatory learning cycle as three phases: (1) forethought, (2) performance, and (3) self-reflection. Each phase has students consider both the learning at hand (the academic or behavioral outcome) and the monitoring of self. Following is an outline of the phases and the general activities students would engage in.

1. **The forethought phase:** Students do a task analysis (set goals and make plans) and reflect on their self-motivational beliefs (reflect on their level of self-efficacy).

2. **The performance phase:** Students exercise self-control (using a variety of management strategies) and engage in self-observation (observing the discrepancy between their current performance and the desirable outcome to potentially make adjustments).

3. **The self-reflection phase:** Students engage in self-evaluation (judge their degree of success after the fact) and self-reaction (judge their degree of satisfaction and any potential responses going forward).

The self-reflection phase then cycles back to the forethought phase, where students then recalibrate goals and outcome expectancies. This cycle can be applied to a short-term process (for example, one lesson) or a long-term one (a semester or quarter).

The symbiotic relationship emerges as the three phases of self-regulation and the three questions of assessment align. The forethought phase is perfectly aligned with the question, Where am I going? The performance phase is perfectly aligned with the question, Where am I now? The self-reflection phase is perfectly aligned with the question, How do I close the gap?

The Approach to Each Phase

During the forethought phase, students are setting goals and determining levels of efficacy, so when it comes to responsibility or any other attribute, students will consider their current status and what constitutes a reasonable goal, given the cycle at hand. A student might, for example, consider strategies for organizing their time during the week or spend time considering how to plan for a project that is to be completed in a few weeks. In other words, they plan for how they will be more responsible. Teachers will likely lead this process more directly early on and then gradually release this process to their students; however, there will be students in every class who already show this level of competence. These students can serve as role models if teachers simply ask them to share how they plan their week or what strategies they use to map out a big project.

For other attributes, goal setting could include how to improve the quality of relationships, how to manage emotions during times of stress and anxiety, how to maintain integrity of character, how to recognize bias, or how to positively contribute to the collective in a collaborative effort. Figure 7.3 highlights some possible guiding questions for each of the SEL competencies through the three phases.

FORETHOUGHT PHASE	PERFORMANCE PHASE	SELF-REFLECTION PHASE
Self-Awareness		
• What are some ways that I can proudly showcase my identity? • What level of belief do I have in my ability to achieve my goals?	• What assets do I have in my life that I can lean on in this moment or during this time? • How can I grow from here?	• What were all the different emotions I felt during that experience? • Did any of my thoughts or actions reflect any previously held prejudices or biases?
Self-Management		
• What strategies will I use to manage my emotions? • What specifically do I hope to develop during this cycle?	• How can I manage my stress levels in this moment? • Am I sticking to my plan, and am I still organized?	• Was I satisfied with my level of self-discipline? • Did I take initiative? Did I take some calculated risks?
Social Awareness		
• How will I ensure I authentically consider others' perspectives? • What are some ways I will authentically express gratitude to others in my group?	• Am I acknowledging and honoring the strengths of others? • Am I showing the appropriate amount of concern for the feelings of others right now?	• Was I as empathetic and compassionate as I'd planned to be? • Did I recognize any unjust actions or situations that arose?

Relationship Skills		
• How will I ensure I always communicate clearly to my peers? • What strategies or protocols will help our team resolve any conflicts should they arise?	• What could I do to strengthen the relationships I currently have? • Am I productively contributing to our collective problem-solving efforts?	• Did I demonstrate appropriate cultural awareness and sensitivity given the diversity of the group? • Did I stand up for others, did I offer to help when others needed it, or both?
Responsible Decision Making		
• How will I ensure I have all the information necessary to make a good decision? • How can I apply the critical-thinking skills I've learned in school to my outside-of-school life?	• Have we exhausted all plausible solutions to the current dilemma? • How open-minded am I being right now?	• Did I ensure I had all the information necessary to make a good decision? • What impact did my decision have on me, my family, my peers, and (possibly) the community?

Sources: CASEL, n.d.b; Zimmerman, 2011.

Figure 7.3: Self-regulation of the five SEL competencies.

The questions in figure 7.3 would have to be contextualized to both the circumstances and the age of the students; these questions are just examples to guide possible processes and protocols that we educators could establish to allow students to self-regulate their social competence. Figure 7.4 (page 142) shows an example of how the reflection questions might be slightly adapted for elementary-aged students.

As for reporting, we could make any of the structures identified in previous chapters (see specifically chapter 6, page 109) student centered and student driven. However, despite the applicability of student self-assessment and reporting, we teachers will need to remain even a small part of the process if only for the purpose of validating the students' self-reflective judgments. It is still critical that what is reported is as accurate as possible.

FORETHOUGHT PHASE	PERFORMANCE PHASE	SELF-REFLECTION PHASE
Self-Awareness		
• What are some ways that I can proudly show people who I am? • Do I believe I can reach my goals?	• What support do I have in my life that I can use to help me in this moment? • How can I get better?	• How did I feel during that experience? • Did any of my thoughts reveal any negative judgments I have about myself?
Self-Management		
• What strategies will I use to make sure my emotions don't negatively impact me? • What habit or skills do I hope to develop this time?	• What is my plan for when I feel stress? • Am I still on track? Am I still organized?	• Am I happy with my self-control? • Did I self-start anything? Did I take any risks?
Social Awareness		
• How will I make sure I hear what others have to say? • How will I show gratitude to others in my group?	• Am I acknowledging and honoring the strengths of others? • Am I showing concern for the feelings of others right now?	• Was I as understanding of how others felt as I'd planned to be? • Did I name and notice any actions or situations that were not right?
Relationship Skills		
• How will I make sure I always communicate clearly to my peers? • What can we do to resolve any conflicts that occur?	• What could I do to strengthen my current relationships? • Am I productively contributing to my team's problem-solving efforts?	• Did I recognize and honor the diversity of the group? • Did I stand up for others or did I offer to help when others needed it?

Responsible Decision Making		
• How will I make sure I have all the information needed to make a good decision? • How can I use what I've learned in school in my life outside of school?	• Have we thought of every possible solution to the current problem we're dealing with? • How open-minded am I being right now?	• Did I make sure I had all the information needed to make a good decision? • How did my decision affect me and my peers?

Sources: CASEL, n.d.b; Zimmerman, 2011.

Figure 7.4: Self-regulation of the five SEL competencies—Elementary-aged students.

Summary

Releasing the responsibility for monitoring and maintaining social competence from teachers to students is the desirable endgame of any schoolwide efforts. Positioning the five SEL competencies as the ends brings an organizational framework that provides a set of internal and external skills for students to develop. Teachers should not interpret the transfer of responsibility as a decrease in importance or focus. Taking a SAFE (sequenced, active, focused, and explicit) approach to the development of these SEL competencies is essential regardless of where the control rests.

To monitor and maintain their social development, students must be well versed in the practices and processes of self- and peer assessment. Using their own expertise, teachers purposefully create opportunities for students to practice and hone the skill of recognizing where they are in relation to where they are going so they can close the gap and continue to grow. In particular, peer assessment allows students to practice their monitoring skills while simultaneously participating in an experience that requires social competence.

The three guiding questions of the assessment cycle provide the substance for students to be more self-regulatory of their social development; the three phases of self-regulation provide the process through which students will actively regulate their social development. Each is a necessary part of the other if the schoolwide effort to release responsibility is going to manifest with any sustainability.

Questions for Learning Teams

1. What quotation or passage encapsulates your main takeaway from this chapter? What immediate action (small, medium, or large) will you take as a result of this takeaway? Explain both to your team.

2. How ready are you to transfer the responsibility of monitoring to students? What do you think needs to happen to increase your readiness? Reflect on your colleagues' readiness and what would increase their readiness as well.

3. What are some successes you've had utilizing self-assessment with your students? What are some challenges you continue to face? Also reflect on some successes and challenges regarding peer assessment.

4. How familiar are you (and your colleagues) with the five SEL competencies? Would incorporating them as the guiding framework within your school context be a simple, moderate, or challenging prospect? Explain.

5. Which of the three phases of self-regulation (forethought, performance, or self-reflection) do you most frequently utilize in your classroom? Which do you least frequently utilize? What ideas do you have for increasing the frequency of all phases?

6. What would your ideal vision be for a comprehensive system (from monitoring to assessment to reporting) where students self-regulate the development of their social competence?

Epilogue

Now that the impact of their efforts is on full display, the faculty at City Center School realizes that the purposeful time and energy they committed to redefining accountability in their building has finally manifested their vision. What had in the beginning felt slightly manufactured and abstract to teachers became the new norm for teaching both academic and social skills. With culturally inclusive norms and trauma-informed processes in place, students were now answerable for their actions and self-reflective about how they could continue to expand their social competence.

Effective implementation of prevention efforts in Tier 1 (teaching, reinforcing, redirecting, and maintaining) led to effectively executed interventions and instruction in Tier 2 for those students who needed supplemental support. And those students who truly need individualized support receive it in Tier 3 by dedicated faculty who have the time, resources, and expertise. Students are holding themselves and their peers accountable, which allows the faculty to guide rather than monitor, to facilitate rather than dictate. Students are self-directed, parents and families have embraced the vision, and stakeholders in the community have come to realize that City Center is truly teaching the whole child.

This is what the future can look like with a purposeful and relentless approach to redefining student accountability and a focus on developing self-directed, self-reflective, socially competent learners. It doesn't happen overnight, and it takes an unwavering belief that once the needs of all learners are met, their social competence will expand. Schools that find their balance and address both the academic and social sides of the learning ledger will develop well-rounded students whose academic competence and social intelligence will serve them in their futures. That balance can only be achieved when a school faculty decides that social skills and behavioral competence are important enough to dedicate the necessary time, energy, and attention that puts how students learn on par with what they are learning.

References and Resources

Ainsworth, L. (2013). *Prioritizing the Common Core: Identifying specific standards to emphasize the most.* Edgewood, CO: Lead + Learn Press.

Aksoy, P., & Gresham, F. M. (2020). Theoretical bases of "social-emotional learning intervention programs" for preschool children. *International Online Journal of Education and Teaching, 7*(4), 1517–1531. Accessed at https://iojet.org/index.php/IOJET/article/view/1010 on August 19, 2022.

Antinluoma, M., Ilomäki, L., Lahti-Nuuttila, P., & Toom, A. (2018). Schools as professional learning communities. *Journal of Education and Learning, 7*(5), 76–91.

Augustine, C. H., Engberg, J., Grimm, G. E., Lee, E., Wang, E. L., Christianson, K., et al. (2018). *Can restorative practices improve school climate and curb suspensions? An evaluation of the impact of restorative practices in a mid-sized urban school district.* RAND Corporation. Accessed at www.rand.org/pubs/research_reports/RR2840.html on January 4, 2023.

Balfanz, R., Herzog, L., & Mac Iver, D. J. (2007). Preventing student disengagement and keeping students on the graduation path in urban middle-grades schools: Early identification and effective interventions. *Educational Psychology, 42*(4), 223–235.

Bear, G. G., Whitcomb, S. A., Elias, M. J., & Blank, J. C. (2015). SEL and schoolwide positive behavioral interventions and supports. In J. A. Durlak, C. E. Domitrovich, R. P. Weissberg, & T. P. Gullotta (Eds), *Handbook of social and emotional learning* (pp. 453–467). New York: Guilford Press.

Black, P. (2013). Formative and summative aspects of assessment: Theoretical and research foundations in the context of pedagogy. In J. H. McMillan (Ed.), *SAGE handbook of research on classroom assessment* (pp. 167–178). Thousand Oaks, CA: SAGE.

Black, P., & Wiliam, D. (1998). Assessment and classroom learning. *Assessment in Education: Principles, Policy and Practice, 5*(1), 7–74.

Bolam, R., McMahon, A., Stoll, L., Thomas, S., & Wallace, M. (2005). *Creating and sustaining effective professional learning communities* (Research Report No. 637). Nottingham, United Kingdom: Department for Education and Skills. Accessed at https://dera.ioe.ac.uk/5622/1/RR637.pdf on August 19, 2022.

Bonner, S. M. (2013). Validity in classroom assessment: Purposes, properties, and principles. In J. H. McMillan (Ed.), *SAGE handbook of research on classroom assessment* (pp. 87–106). Thousand Oaks, CA: SAGE.

Brackett, M. A., Elbertson, N. A., & Rivers, S. E. (2015). *Applying theory to the development of approaches to SEL.* In J. A. Durlak, C. E. Domitrovich, R. P. Weissberg, & T. P. Gullotta (Eds), *Handbook of social and emotional learning* (pp. 20–32). New York: Guilford Press.

Bradshaw, C. P., Pas, E. T., Debnam, K. J., & Johnson, S. L. (2015). A focus on implementation of positive behavioral interventions and supports (PBIS) in high schools: Associations with bullying and other indicators of school disorder. *School Psychology Review, 44*(4), 480–498.

Bradshaw, C. P., Waasdorp, T. E., & Leaf, P. J. (2012). Effects of school-wide positive behavioral interventions and supports on child behavior problems. *Pediatrics, 130*(5), 1136–1145.

Brennan, R. L. (1998). Misconceptions at the intersection of measurement theory and practice. *Educational Measurement: Issues and Practice, 17*(1), 5–9.

Brighton, K. L. (2007). *Coming of age: The education and development of young adolescents.* Westerville, OH: National Middle School Association.

Brookhart, S. M. (2013). Classroom assessment in the context of motivation theory and research. In J. H. McMillan (Ed.), *SAGE handbook of research on classroom assessment* (pp. 35–54). Thousand Oaks, CA: SAGE.

Brookhart, S. M., & Guskey, T. R. (2019). Reliability in grading and grading scales. In T. R. Guskey & S. M. Brookhart (Eds.), *What we know about grading: What works, what doesn't, and what's next* (pp. 13–31). Alexandria, VA: ASCD.

Brown, G. T. L., & Harris, L. R. (2013). Student self-assessment. In J. H. McMillan (Ed.), *SAGE handbook of research on classroom assessment* (pp. 367–393). Thousand Oaks, CA: SAGE.

Bruhn, A. L., Gorsh, J., Hannan, C., & Hirsch, S. E. (2014). Simple strategies for reflecting on and responding to common criticisms of PBIS. *Journal of Special Education Leadership, 27*(1), 13–25.

Buffum, A., & Mattos, M. (2022). *RTI at Work.* Accessed at www.solutiontree.com/ca/rti-at-work /why-rti-at-work on January 4, 2023.

Buffum, A., Mattos, M., & Malone, J. (2018). *Taking action: A handbook for RTI at Work.* Bloomington, IN: Solution Tree Press.

Buffum, A., Mattos, M., & Weber, C. (2011). *Simplifying response to intervention: Four essential guiding principles.* Bloomington, IN: Solution Tree Press.

Camera, L. (2020, October 13). School suspension data shows glaring disparities in discipline by race. *U.S. News & World Report.* Accessed at https://www.usnews.com/news/education-news/articles /2020-10-13/school-suspension-data-shows-glaring-disparities-in-discipline-by-race on March 3, 2023.

Canada Without Poverty. (n.d.). *Just the facts.* Accessed at https://cwp-csp.ca/poverty/just-the-facts on August 22, 2022.

Canadian Mental Health Association. (2021, July 19). *Fast facts about mental health and mental illness.* Accessed at https://cmha.ca/brochure/fast-facts-about-mental-illness on August 22, 2022.

Caskey, M., & Anfara, V. A., Jr. (2014, October). *Developmental characteristics of young adolescents.* Accessed at www.amle.org/research/developmental-characteristics-of-young-adolescents on August 22, 2022.

Center for Emotional Education. (2017, May 5). *There is no misbehavior* [Blog post]. Accessed at https://centerforemotionaleducation.com/blog/2017/5/5/there-is-no-misbehavior on November 21, 2022.

Center on Positive Behavioral Interventions and Supports. (2023). *Tier 2.* Accessed at www.pbis.org /pbis/tier-2 on December 20, 2022.

Centers for Disease Control and Prevention. (2022). *Fast facts: Preventing adverse childhood experiences*. Accessed at https://cdc.gov/violenceprevention/aces/fastfact.html on August 23, 2022.

Chapman, C., Laird, J., Ifill, N., & KewalRamani, A. (2011, October). *Trends in high school dropout and completion rates in the United States: 1972–2009* (NCES 2012-006). Washington, DC: National Center for Education Statistics. Accessed at https://nces.ed.gov/pubs2012/2012006.pdf on August 22, 2022.

Chappuis, J. (2014). *Seven strategies of assessment for learning* (2nd ed.). Portland, OR: Pearson.

Child Mind Institute. (2018). *Understanding anxiety in children and teens*. Accessed at https://childmind.org/awareness-campaigns/childrens-mental-health-report/2018-childrens-mental-health-report on December 4, 2022.

Collaborative for Academic, Social, and Emotional Learning. (n.d.a). *What is social and emotional learning?* Accessed at https://drc.casel.org/what-is-sel on August 22, 2022.

Collaborative for Academic, Social, and Emotional Learning. (n.d.b). *What is the CASEL framework?* Accessed at https://casel.org/fundamentals-of-sel/what-is-the-casel-framework on August 23, 2022.

Conference Board of Canada. (2022, July 28). *Employability skills*. Accessed at https://www.conferenceboard.ca/product/employability-skills/. on March 2, 2023.

Covey, S. R. (2020). *The seven habits of highly effective people: Powerful lessons in personal change* (30th anniversary ed.). New York: Simon & Schuster.

Darling-Hammond, L. (2015). Social and emotional learning: Critical skills for building healthy schools. In J. A. Durlak, C. E. Domitrovich, R. P. Weissberg, & T. P. Gullotta (Eds.), *Handbook of social and emotional learning: Research and practice* (pp. xi–xiv). New York: Guilford Press.

Darling-Hammond, S., Fronius, T. A., Sutherland, H., Guckenburg, S., Petrosino, A., & Hurley, N. (2020). Effectiveness of restorative justice in U.S. K–12 schools: A review of quantitative research. *Contemporary School Psychology*, *24*(3), 295–308.

Davies, M., & Cooper, G. (2013). Training teachers to target and develop social skills as an academic enabler. In B. Knight & R. Van Der Zwan (Eds.), *Teaching innovations supporting student outcomes in the 21st century* (pp. 45–55). Tarragindi, Queensland, Australia: Oxford Global Press.

Desautels, L. (2018). *Aiming for discipline instead of punishment: Brain-aligned discipline isn't compliance-driven or punitive—it's about supporting students in creating sustainable changes in behavior*. Accessed at www.edutopia.org/article/aiming-discipline-instead-punishment on January 4, 2023.

Dimich, N., Erkens, C., & Schimmer, T. (2023). *Jackpot! Nurturing student investment through assessment*. Bloomington, IN: Solution Tree Press.

Dixon, C. (2004). Plus/minus grading: If given a choice. *College students journal*, *38*(2), 280.

Dobbs, D. (2011, October). Beautiful brains. *National Geographic*, *220*(4), 36–59.

DuFour, R. (2011). Work together: But only if you want to. *Phi Delta Kappan*, *92*(5), 57–61.

DuFour, R., DuFour, R., Eaker, R., Many, T. W., & Mattos, M. (2016). *Learning by doing: A handbook for Professional Learning Communities at Work* (3rd ed.). Bloomington, IN: Solution Tree Press.

DuFour, R., & Eaker, R. (1998). *Professional Learning Communities at Work: Best practices for enhancing student achievement*. Bloomington, IN: Solution Tree Press.

DuFour, R., & Reeves, D. (2016). The futility of PLC lite. *Phi Delta Kappan*, *97*(6), 69–71.

Durlak, J. A., Weissberg, R. P., Dymnicki, A. B., Taylor, R. D., & Schellinger, K. B. (2011). The impact of enhancing students' social and emotional learning: A meta-analysis of school-based universal interventions. *Child Development*, *82*(1), 405–432.

Elliott, S. N., Frey, J. R., & Davies, M. (2015). Systems for assessing and improving students' social skills to achieve academic competence. In J. A. Durlak, C. E. Domitrovich, R. P. Weissberg, & T. P. Gullotta (Eds.), *Handbook of social and emotional learning: Research and practice* (pp. 301–319). New York: Guilford Press.

Erkens, C. (2016). *Collaborative common assessments: Teamwork. Instruction. Results.* Bloomington, IN: Solution Tree Press.

Erkens, C., Schimmer, T., & Dimich, N. (2017). *Essential assessment: Six tenets for bringing hope, efficacy, and achievement to the classroom.* Bloomington, IN: Solution Tree Press.

Freeman, J., Simonsen, B., McCoach, D. B., Sugai, G., Lombardi, A., & Horner, R. H. (2016). Relationship between school-wide positive behavior interventions and supports and academic, attendance, and behavior outcomes in high schools. *Journal of Positive Behavior Interventions, 18*(1), 41–51.

Fullan, M. (2015). *The new meaning of educational change* (5th ed.). New York: Teachers College Press.

Gomez, J. A., Rucinski, C. L., & Higgins-D'Alessandro, A. (2021). Promising pathways from school restorative practices to educational equity. *Journal of Moral Education, 50*(4), 452–470.

González, T. (2015). Socializing schools: Addressing racial disparities in discipline through restorative justice. In D. Losen (Ed.), *Closing the school discipline gap: Equitable remedies for excessive exclusion* (pp. 151–165). New York: Teachers College Press.

Greenberg, M. T., Katz, D. A., & Klein, L. C. (2015). The potential effects of SEL on biomarkers and health outcomes. In J. A. Durlak, C. E. Domitrovich, R. P. Weissberg, & T. P. Gullotta (Eds.), *Handbook of social and emotional learning: Research and practice* (pp. 81–96). New York: Guilford Press.

Gregory, A., Clawson, K., Davis, A., & Gerewitz, J. (2016). The promise of restorative practices to transform teacher–student relationships and achieve equity in school discipline. *Journal of Educational and Psychological Consultation, 26*(4), 325–353.

Gregory, A., Huang, F. L., Anyon, Y., Greer, E., & Downing, B. (2018). An examination of restorative interventions and racial equity in out-of-school suspensions. *School Psychology Review, 47*(2), 167–182.

Gresham, F. M. (2002). Best practices in social skills training. In A. Thomas, & J. Grimes (Eds.), *Best practices in school psychology IV* (pp. 1029–1040). Bethesda, MD: National Association of School Psychologists.

GuardChild. (n.d.). *Cyber bullying statistics.* Accessed at www.guardchild.com/cyber-bullying-statistics on August 22, 2022.

Gulbrandson, K. (2019, June 27). *Trends in social-emotional learning research: What are the outcomes?* [Blog post]. Accessed at https://cfchildren.org/blog/2019/06/trends-in-social-emotional-learning -research-what-are-the-outcomes on August 22, 2022.

Guskey, T. R. (2015). *On your mark: Challenging the conventions of grading and reporting.* Bloomington, IN: Solution Tree Press.

Hammond, Z. (2015). *Culturally responsive teaching and the brain: Promoting authentic engagement and rigor among culturally and linguistically diverse students.* Thousand Oaks, CA: Corwin.

Hannigan, J., & Hannigan, J. (2016). Comparison of traditional and innovative discipline beliefs in administrators. *Journal for Leadership, Equity, and Research, 3*(1), 39–46.

Hannigan, J., Hannigan, J., Mattos, M., & Buffum, A. (2021). *Behavior solutions: Teaching academic and social skills through RTI at Work.* Bloomington, IN: Solution Tree Press.

Hargreaves, A. (2007). Sustainable professional learning communities. In L. Stoll & K. S. Louis (Eds.), *Professional learning communities: Divergence, depth and dilemmas* (pp. 181–196). Maidenhead, United Kingdom: Open University Press.

Hargreaves, A., & Fink, D. (2006). Redistributed leadership for sustainable professional learning communities. *Journal of School Leadership, 16*(5), 550–565.

Hargreaves, A., & Fullan, M. (2012). *Professional capital: Transforming teaching in every school.* New York: Teachers College Press.

Harris, A. (2011). System improvement through collective capacity building. *Journal of Educational Administration, 49*(6), 624–636.

Hattie, J. A. C. (2009). *Visible learning: A synthesis of over 800 meta-analyses relating to achievement.* New York: Routledge.

Hattie, J. A. C. (2018). *Hattie ranking: 252 Influences and effect sizes related to student achievement.* Accessed at https://visible-learning.org/hattie-ranking-influences-effect-sizes-learning-achievement/ on December 15, 2022.

Hattie, J. A. C., & Timperley, H. (2007). The power of feedback. *Review of Educational Research, 77*(1), 81–112.

Heritage, M. (2021). *Formative assessment: Making it happen in the classroom* (2nd ed.). Thousand Oaks, CA: Corwin Press.

Hirsch, S. E., Bruhn, A. L., Randall, K., Dunn, M., Shelnut, J., & Lloyd, J. W. (2020). Developing and implementing FBA-BIPs in elementary classrooms: A conceptual replication. *The Journal of Special Education Apprenticeship, 9*(2), 1–25.

Horner, R. H., & Sugai, G. (2015). School-wide PBIS: An example of applied behavior analysis implemented at a scale of social importance. *Behavior Analysis in Practice, 8*(1), 80–85.

Horner, R. H., Sugai, G., & Anderson, C. M. (2010). Examining the evidence base for school-wide positive behavior support. *Focus on Exceptional Children, 42*(8), 1–14.

Kane, M. (2011). The errors of our ways. *Journal of Educational Measurement, 48*(1), 12–30.

Kanter, R. M. (2004). *Confidence: How winning streaks and losing streaks begin and end.* New York: Crown Business.

Karaman, P. (2021). The impact of self-assessment on academic performance: A meta-analysis study. *International Journal of Research in Education and Science, 7*(4), 1151–1166.

Kaya, I. (2020). Investigation of the relationship between children's prosocial behaviour and self-regulation skills. *Cypriot Journal of Educational Science, 15*(5), 877–886.

Kessler, R. C., Chiu, W. T., Demler, O., Merikangas, K. R., & Walters, E. E. (2005). Prevalence, severity, and comorbidity of 12-month DSM-IV disorders in the National Comorbidity Survey Replication. *Archives of General Psychiatry, 62*(6), 617–627.

King, B. (2020). How long does it take to for a new habit? Why changing our behavior is so difficult. *Psychology Today.* Accessed at https://www.psychologytoday.com/us/blog/taking-it-easy/202001/how-long-does-it-take-form-new-habit on March 1, 2023.

Khalifa, M. (2018). *Culturally responsive school leadership.* Cambridge, MA: Harvard Education Press.

Kluger, A. N., & DeNisi, A. (1996). The effects of feedback interventions on performance: A historical review, a meta-analysis, and a preliminary feedback intervention theory. *Psychological Bulletin, 119*(2), 254–284.

Kremer, K. P., Flower, A., Huang, J., & Vaughn, M. G. (2016). Behavior problems and children's academic achievement: A test of growth-curve models with gender and racial differences. *Children and Youth Services Review, 67*, 95–104.

Lawrence, A. A. S., & Saileela, K. (2019). Self-concept and self-regulation of higher secondary students. *Journal on Educational Psychology, 13*(1), 45–53.

Lewis, T. (2014). *Essential elements of social skills instruction as a Tier II intervention.* Accessed at www.slideserve.com/mora/essential-elements-of-social-skill-instruction-as-a-tier-ii-intervention on February 20, 2022.

Little, J. W. (2011). Professional community and professional development in the learning-centered school. In M. Kooy & K. van Veen (Eds.), *Teacher learning that matters: International perspectives* (pp. 22–43). New York: Routledge.

Loman, S., Strickland-Cohen, M. K., Borgmeier, C., & Horner, R. (n.d.). *Basic FBA to BSP: Trainer's manual*. Accessed at https://assets-global.website-files.com/5d3725188825e071f1670246/5db71e5e6b872d07100ac4c5_TrainerManual.pdf on December 20, 2022.

Lomos, C. (2017). To what extent do teachers in European countries differ in their professional community practices? *School Effectiveness and School Improvement, 28*(2), 276–291.

Maag, J. W. (2001). Rewarded by punishment: Reflections on the disuse of positive reinforcement in schools. *Exceptional Children, 67*(2), 173–186.

Manion, L. (2020, September 21). *What safety means as a trauma survivor* [Blog post]. Accessed at https://nami.org/Blogs/NAMI-Blog/September-2020/What-Safety-Means-as-a-Trauma-Survivor on August 23, 2022.

McFarland, J., Cui, J., Holmes, J., & Wang, X. (2020). *Trends in high school dropout and completion rates in the United States: 2019*. Accessed at https://nces.ed.gov/pubs2020/2020117.pdf on March 2, 2023.

Menzies, F. (2018). *Nine cultural value differences you need to know*. Accessed at https://cultureplusconsulting.com/2015/06/23/nine-cultural-value-differences-you-need-to-know on August 23, 2022.

Merikangas, K. R., He, J., Burstein, M., Swendsen, J., Avenevoli, S., Case, B., et al. (2011). Service utilization for lifetime mental disorders in U.S. adolescents: Results of the National Comorbidity Survey–Adolescent Supplement (NCS–A). *Journal of the American Academy of Child and Adolescent Psychiatry, 50*(1), 32–45.

Morrison, B. (2015). Restorative justice in education: Changing lenses on education's three Rs. *Restorative Justice, 3*(3), 445–452.

Moulakdi, A., & Bouchamma, Y. (2020). Elementary schools working as professional learning communities: Effects on student learning. *International Education Studies, 13*(6), 1–13.

National Center for Education Statistics. (2019). *Bullying: Fast facts*. Accessed at https://nces.ed.gov/fastfacts/display.asp?id=719 on December 4, 2022.

National Coalition for Core Arts Standards. (2014, May 29). *National Core Arts Standards*. Accessed at www.nationalartsstandards.org/content/develop-1 on August 22, 2022.

Organization for Economic Cooperation and Development. (2021). *Poverty rate*. Accessed at https://data.oecd.org/inequality/poverty-rate.htm on December 15, 2022.

Parkes, J. (2013). Reliability in classroom assessment. In J. H. McMillan (Ed.), *SAGE handbook of research on classroom assessment* (pp. 107–123). Thousand Oaks, CA: SAGE.

Paterson, G. D. (2019). Improving student learning through professional learning communities: Employing a system-wide approach. *Canadian Journal for New Scholars in Education, 10*(1), 42–48.

Peguero, A. A., Varela, K. S., Marchbanks, M. P., Blake, J., & Eason, J. M. (2018). School punishment and education: Racial/ethnic disparities with grade retention and the role of urbanicity. *Urban education, 56*(2), 228–260.

Perry, B. D., & Winfrey, O. (2021). *What happened to you? Conversations on trauma, resilience, and healing*. New York: Flatiron Books.

Perry, B. L., & Morris, E. W. (2014). Suspending progress: Collateral consequences of exclusionary punishment in public schools. *American Sociological Review, 79*(6), 1067–1087. https://doi.org/10.1177/0003122414556308

Pink, D. H. (2009). *Drive: The surprising truth about what motivates us*. New York: Riverhead Books.

Pintrich, P. R., & Zusho, A. (2002). The development of academic self-regulation: The role of cognitive and motivational factors. In A. Wigfield & J. S. Eccles (Eds.), *Development of achievement motivation* (pp. 249–284). San Diego, CA: Academic Press.

Ratcliffe, C. (2015, September). *Child poverty and adult success*. Washington, DC: Urban Institute. Accessed at https://urban.org/sites/default/files/publication/65766/2000369-Child-Poverty-and-Adult-Success.pdf on August 22, 2022.

Richmond, G., & Manokore, V. (2011). Identifying elements critical for functional and sustainable professional learning communities. *Science Education, 95*(3), 543–570.

Robbins, M. M., Onodipe, G., & Marks, A. (2020). Reflective writing and self-regulated learning in multidisciplinary flipped classrooms. *Journal of the Scholarship of Teaching and Learning, 20*(3), 20–32.

Ruiz-Primo, M. A., & Li, M. (2013). Examining formative feedback in the classroom context: New research perspectives. In J. H. McMillan (Ed.), *SAGE handbook of research on classroom assessment* (pp. 215–232). Thousand Oaks, CA: SAGE.

Sadler, D. R. (1989). Formative assessment and the design of instructional systems. *Instructional Science, 18*(2), 119–144.

Schimmer, T. (2016). *Grading from the inside out: Bringing accuracy to student assessment through a standards-based mindset*. Bloomington, IN: Solution Tree Press.

SHAPE America. (2013). *National standards for K–12 physical education*. Reston, VA: Author. Accessed at https://shapeamerica.org/standards/pe on August 22, 2022.

Shute, V. J. (2008). Focus on formative feedback. *Review of Educational Research, 78*(1), 153–189.

Shweta, B., Bajpal, H., & Chaturvedi, H. (2015). Evaluation of inter-rater agreement and inter-rater reliability for observational data: An overview of concepts and methods. *Journal of the Indian Academy of Applied Psychology, 41*(3), 20–27.

Simpson, A. (2017). The misdirection of public policy: Comparing and combining standardised effect sizes. *Journal of Education Policy, 32*(4), 450–466.

Slavin, R. (2018, June 21). *John Hattie is wrong* [Blog post]. Accessed at https://robertslavinsblog.wordpress.com/2018/06/21/john-hattie-is-wrong on August 22, 2022.

Sleegers, P., den Brok, P., Verbiest, E., Moolenaar, N. M., & Daly, A. J. (2013). Toward conceptual clarity: A multidimensional, multilevel model of professional learning communities in Dutch elementary schools. *Elementary School Journal, 114*(1), 118–137.

Stobart, G. (2018). Becoming proficient: An alternative perspective on the role of feedback. In A. Anastasiya, A. Lipnevich, & J. Smith (Eds.), *The Cambridge handbook of instructional feedback* (pp. 29–51). Cambridge, United Kingdom: Cambridge University Press.

Stoll, L., Bolam, R., & Greenwood, A. (2007). *Professional learning communities: Divergence, depth and dilemmas*. Maidenhead, United Kingdom: Open University Press.

Substance Abuse and Mental Health Services Administration. (n.d.). *Understanding child trauma*. Accessed at https://samhsa.gov/child-trauma/understanding-child-trauma on August 23, 2022.

Sugai, G., Lewis-Palmer, T., & Hagan-Burke, S. (2000). Overview of the functional behavioral assessment process. *Exceptionality, 8*(3), 149–160.

Sugai, G., & Simonsen, B. (2020). Reinforcement foundations of a function-based behavioral approach for students with challenging behavior. *Beyond Behavior, 29*(2), 78–85.

Tatum, B. D. (2017). *Why are all the Black kids sitting together in the cafeteria? And other conversations about race* (20th anniversary ed.). New York: Basic Books.

Thienpermpool, P. (2021). Teachers' practice and perceptions of self-assessment and peer assessment of presentation skills. *English Language Teaching, 14*(12), 183–188.

Topping, K. (2013). Peers as a source of formative and summative assessment. In J. H. McMillan (Ed.), *SAGE handbook of research on classroom assessment* (pp. 395–412). Thousand Oaks, CA: SAGE.

Topping, K. J. (2013). Peers as a source of formative and summative assessment. In J. H. McMillan (Ed.), *SAGE handbook of research on classroom assessment* (pp. 395–412). Thousand Oaks, CA: SAGE.

Trout, L. (2021). *The toolkit before the toolkit: Centering adaptive and relational elements of restorative practices for implementation success.* San Francisco: WestEd. Accessed at https://selcenter.wested.org /wp-content/uploads/sites/3/2022/03/SEL_Restorative-Practices-Guide-5.pdf on August 23, 2022.

Tyler, T. (2006). Restorative justice and procedural justice: Dealing with rule breaking. *Journal of Social Issues, 62*(2), 307–326.

U.S. Census Bureau. (2014). *Current population survey: Annual social and economic supplement.* Washington, DC: Author.

U.S. Census Bureau. (2022). *Current population survey: Annual social and economic (ASEC) supplement.* Washington, DC: Author.

Valenzuela, J. (2021, October 14). *5 trauma-informed strategies for supporting refugee students.* Edutopia. Accessed at https://www.edutopia.org/article/5-trauma-informed-strategies-supporting-refugee -students/ on March 2, 2023.

Van Camp, A. M., Wehby, J. H., Copeland, B. A., & Bruhn, A. L. (2021). Building from the bottom up: The importance of Tier 1 supports in the context of Tier 2 interventions. *Journal of Positive Behavior Interventions, 23*(1), 53–64. https://doi.org/10.1177/1098300720916716

Vescio, V., Ross, D., & Adams, A. (2008). A review of research on the impact of professional learning communities on teaching practice and student learning. *Teaching and Teacher Education, 24*(1), 80–91.

Warnick, B. R., & Scribner, C. F. (2020). Discipline, punishment, and the moral community of schools. *Theory and Research in Education, 18*(1), 98–116.

Weisinger, H., & Pawliw-Fry, J. P. (2015). *Performing under pressure: The science of doing your best when it matters most.* New York: Crown Business.

Weissberg, R. P., Durlak, J. A., Domitrovich, C. E., & Gullotta, T. P. (2015). *Social and emotional learning: Past, present, & future.* In J. A. Durlak, C. E. Domitrovich, R. P. Weissberg, & T. P. Gullotta (Eds.), *Handbook of social and emotional learning: Research and practice* (pp. 3–19). New York: Guilford Press.

Wiliam, D. (2016). *Leadership for teacher learning: Creating a culture where all teachers improve so that all students succeed.* West Palm Beach, FL: Learning Sciences International.

Williams, R., Brien, K., Sprague, C., & Sullivan, G. (2008). Professional learning communities: Developing a school-level readiness instrument. *Canadian Journal of Educational Administration and Policy, 74.* Accessed at https://journalhosting.ucalgary.ca/index.php/cjeap/issue/view/2905 on August 22, 2022.

Winne, P. H. (2011). A cognitive and metacognitive analysis of self-regulated learning. In B. J. Zimmerman & D. H. Schunk (Eds.), *Handbook of self-regulation of learning and performance* (pp. 15–32). New York: Routledge.

Wnuk, A. (2018). *When the brain starts adulting.* Accessed at www.brainfacts.org/thinking-sensing-and -behaving/aging/2018/when-the-brain-starts-adulting-112018 on January 4, 2023.

Zimmerman, B. J. (2011). Motivational sources and outcomes of self-regulated learning and performance. In B. J. Zimmerman & D. H. Schunk (Eds.), *Handbook of self-regulation of learning and performance* (pp. 49–64). New York: Routledge.

Index

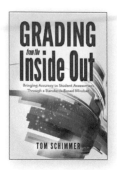

Grading From the Inside Out
Tom Schimmer

The time for grading reform is now. Discover the steps your team can take to implement standards-based practices that transform grading and reporting schoolwide.

BKF646

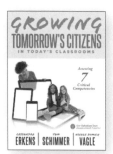

Growing Tomorrow's Citizens
Nicole Dimich, Cassandra Erkens, and Tom Schimmer

Promote student mastery of essential 21st century skills, including collaboration, critical and creative thinking, digital citizenship, and more. Learn the qualities of the most important soft skills and how we can assess and measure them.

BKF765

Jackpot
Nicole Dimich, Cassandra Erkens, and Tom Schimmer

A shift in the educator's mindset is needed to inspire student engagement and create a positive learning experience. *Jackpot!* offers immediate actions and addresses the mindset shift teachers must make to truly achieve student investment in their classrooms.

BKF769

Instructional Agility
Nicole Dimich, Cassandra Erkens, and Tom Schimmer

Discover how to become instructionally agile—moving seamlessly among instruction, formative assessment, and feedback—to enhance student engagement, proficiency, and ownership of learning.

BKF764